DUBLIN

Donated to

**Visual Art Degree
Sherkin Island**

D1493440

LIBRARY
D.I.T. MOUNTJOY S

LIBRARY

D·I·T DUBLIN INSTITUTE
of T

DIT Library Mountjoy Sq

LIBRARY
D.I.T. MOUNTJOY SQ.

Poltrona
Frau

Decio Giulio Riccardo Carugati

LIBRARY
D.I.T. MOUNTJOY SQ.

Poltrona Frau

Timeless, in Time

Electa

Cover
Detail of Vanity Fair,
the replica of the 904 armchair
of 1930

Translation
Christopher Evans

© 2000 by Siae

© 2000 by Electa, Milan
Elemond Editori Associati
All rights reserved

LIBRARY
D.I.T. MOUNTJOY SQ.

Although he drew his inspiration from the Victorian tradition, Renzo Frau's models of armchairs and couches are distinguished by the more balanced definition of their form, the quality of their materials and the care taken over their construction. He also placed an emphasis on comfort and sober elegance, choosing leather as the principal material for covering his furniture. Right from the start, therefore, Frau set standards for refined upholstery, made with consummate manual skill. In fact, after the sudden and premature death of its founder in 1926, the company called Poltrona Frau was able, over the course of its brief and successful management by his widow, Savina Pisati, to go on producing models of undoubted quality. An example of this is the 904 of 1930— our replica of it has been given the name Vanity Fair—a true archetype of the modern armchair and one which has become a symbol of the company in its advertising. To an even greater extent today, however, Poltrona Frau takes pride in and cultivates the heritage of its craftsmanship. In fact the principal concern of the president, Franco Moschini, ever since he took the company over in 1962 and transferred it from Turin to Tolentino, has been, in addition to the laborious salvage of what little remained in the archives to bear witness to the history of the enterprise, a determination to re-create, in a new environment, that school of manual skill, of expert upholstery, first established by Renzo Frau. And at Tolentino, Poltrona Frau has flourished again, leaving behind it forever the long years of stagnancy: today the company is an internationally recognized leader in the sector of leather-upholstered furniture. Its absolutely artisan character allows it to take the best possible approach to advanced industrial technologies and methods, encouraging a research targeted at maintaining a constant level of quality in the product. The designers who collaborate with us, and they include some of the most famous names in the world, know us well: as partners with a strong and determined personality. Designing for Poltrona Frau means above all understanding and preserving the firm's identity. This is only apparently a constraint: in reality, when the design turns out to be a sharing of energies, this fully repays the commitment made by the designer to the company and by the company to the designer. The product becomes a piece in a mosaic and joins other pieces already in the collection: pieces of furniture branded with the Poltrona Frau trademark, the only signature still capable of guaranteeing their quality.

Giancarla Quacquarini
Sales, image and advertising executive Poltrona Frau

LIBRARY
D.I.T. MOUNTJOY SQ.

Poltrona Frau was born as a fairytale, part of Renzo's fairytale. And as a fairytale it has been reborn, like "a prince awakening the sleeping beauty and making her his bride." For here the story really does take the form of a fable: a young Sardinian, Renzo Frau, arrives on the mainland and issues a challenge to the more obsequious forms of eclecticism, defining instead the armchair as a place to be lived in, a soft and sensual object covered with leather, tempting in the fullness of its physical nature. And his models soon set a trend in the most exclusive of interior decorations. Yet "the beauty" fell asleep and slumbered for many long years. She might never have awakened, curled up in that armchair: the 904, whose replica is now called Vanity Fair, which brought together, posthumously, the most innovative of Renzo's intentions. And then came "a prince who fell in love": Franco Moschini took that intention further, first of all reproducing the Frau classics, for he had no desire to break the thread of continuity that he had so laboriously picked up again, and then expanding the front of "timeless" pieces of furniture. To do this, he turned to designers whom he felt to be most respectful of Poltrona Frau's tradition of craftsmanship. And he ventured into other, exclusive realms of furnishing: Residential, Contract, the Car Division. In accepting the publisher's invitation to write this book, my aim has been to cover the whole arc of the company's history, picking out the fundamental models and looking for the contribution made to them first by Franco Moschini and then by his collaborators, designers and all the other people—writers, philosophers, poets and historians— who may have helped to shape the story. If I have not been able to mention all those who have played a part in the fairytale, they nevertheless constitute the essential humus on which I have drawn. In this connection I recall with fondness Silvano Bonfranceschi, Anaide Cantolacqua, Rosalba Luconi, Graziano Marzioni and Antonio Muccichini at Poltrona Frau. In Renzo's time, the places furnished by Frau extended to the interiors of Vincenzo Lancia's prestigious automobiles, convertibles custom built by Pinin Farina, the rooms of grand hotels in the Ciga chain, the first-class decks of transatlantic liners. Today, their equivalents are to be found in those insuperable red Ferraris from Maranello, in the hemicycle of the European Parliament in Strasbourg, in the replica of the 128, from 1919, and in the Donald, the most recent creation, born in 2000. I would like to thank Dario Tagliabue for the care he has taken in making up the illustrations of the most significant and timeless objects, the Poltrona Frau upholstered furniture. My thanks also go to Valentina Lindon, Simona Oreglia, Giacomo Merli, Lucia Impelluso and, in the person of Stefano Peccatori, the whole editorial staff at Electa.

Decio Giulio Riccardo Carugati

Contents

LIBRARY
D.I.T. MOUNTJOY SQ.

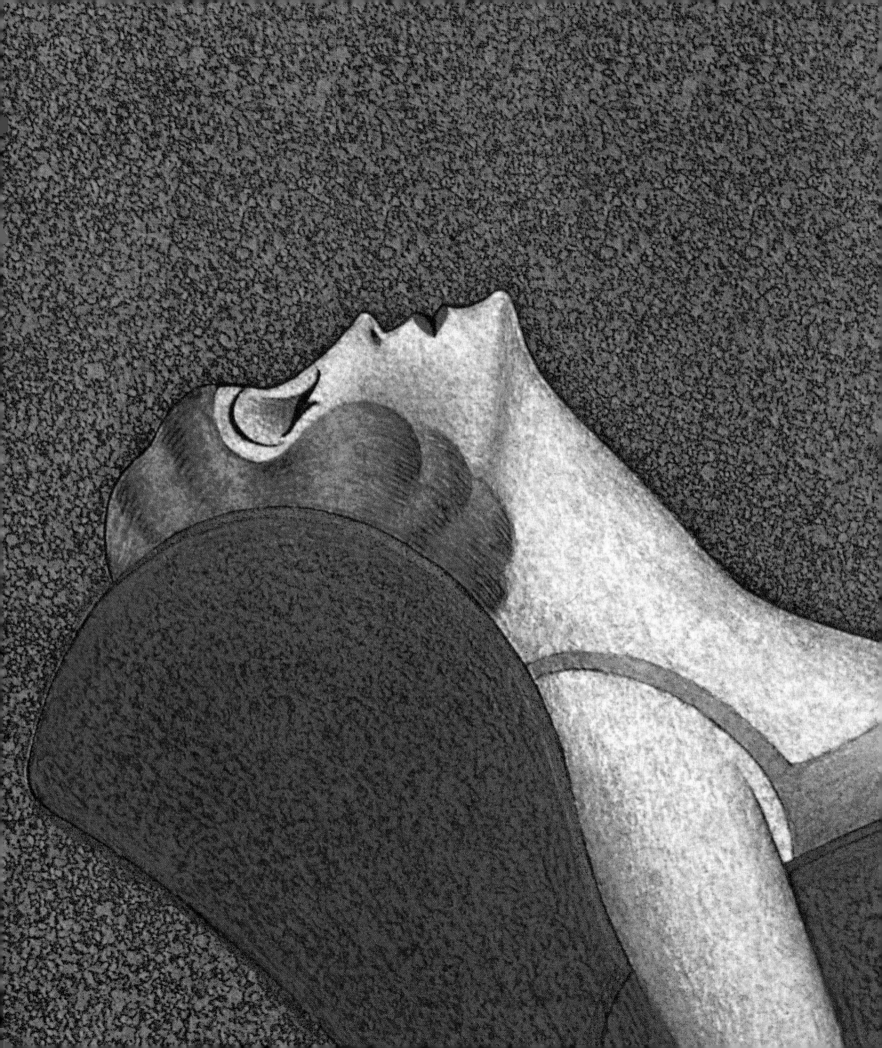

A Fairytale

A traveler by the name of Gaston Charles Vuiller, one of those *Nineteenth-Century Travelers in Sardinia*, adds just one more touch of color to his portrait of Cagliari. "It has the silhouette of a gigantic bird taking flight for Tunisia. Immense marshes ring the city and the Golfo degli Angeli cradles its radiant days and beautiful nights in the melodious murmur of the waves." The writer wanders through the landscape, pausing here and there. "Often I used to climb up sloping streets and alleys to the little square that stands on the edge of the upper quarter... I saw, sometimes, magnificent sunsets: Monte Santo and the Iglesias chain were immersed in a pur-

the date of his birth as for the literary genre in which he expressed himself. "Born perhaps at Perpignan in 1847 or at Ginclé in 1846, he died at Gimel (Corrèze) in 1915. He was a landscape painter and a fine draftsman, illustrating several works by Chateaubriand and Mérimée, winning various prizes for painting, exhibiting at the Salon in Paris and writing articles and essays for magazines. In 1891 he went to the Balearic Islands, Corsica and Sardinia on behalf of the *Journal de voyages* and dedicated several articles to the islands that he visited. The result was a charming book, filled with his impressions, *Les îles oubliées – Les Baléares, la Corse*

Portrait of Renzo Frau at the time of his military service in Milan. View of Cagliari by Guglielmo Bilancioni at the end of the nineteenth century–beginning of the twentieth century.

plish haze in which the planes were dissolved, the sky glowed with gold and a few gleams of light struck a peak and slid like molten metal onto the Campidano."

As a child, perhaps Renzo would sometimes run shouting with his friends along steep streets and alleys, only to fall silent when they reached the top, their eyes wide with amazement at the sight of those mountains turning purple at sunset. As for Vuiller, he was, as the scrupulous and enthusiastic essayist Alberto Boscolo (1920–87) observes, the last genuine traveler of the nineteenth century. Not so much for

et la Sardaigne – Impressions de voyage, published in Paris by Hachette in 1893. The illustrated pages of the book reflect the artist's spirit, his ability to pick out the best things." In fact, as Boscolo points out, it was the genre of pictorial narrative that died out at the turn of the nineteenth century. "Later visitors adapted to a new fashion, a tendency to present a picture of the island's economy and reflect the spirit of its people." In other words they were more interested in a psychological interpretation of the island setting than in representing its outlines.

749   33333 01 0049233

La solenne inaugurazione della nostra Esposizione Internazionale su «La Stampa» del 30 aprile 1911.

Born in 1880, Lorenzo Frau, Renzo to his family from the start, was eleven years old when Vuiller painted that "last touch of color on the island," his portrait of the city. And he had already left Cagliari for the mainland when, "unlike other travelers—rhapsodizing about sculpted stones and painted colors—J.E. Crawford Flitch, who had spent time on the Balearic Islands and arrived in Sardinia at the beginning of the twentieth century, was an explorer of human beings and their moods. Alert and perceptive, he wrote a book entitled *Mediterranean Moods; Foot-Notes of Travel in the Islands of Mallorca, Menorca, Ibiza and Sardinia* that was published

spills its teeming life… The rooms of the hovels, both bedrooms and living rooms, and they are frequently one and the same, open onto the streets and the streets open into them. You are invited in to see the bed that is never made and the meal that has not yet been cleared away. All the household chores, cooking, washing, scrubbing, peeling potatoes, nursing children, sewing undergarments, are carried out in public. The children slink out of the door in the scantiest of clothing; the men sleep on the ground and, in their waking moments, approve or criticize the women's work. The most private matters are discussed eloquently

The International Exposition in Turin, 1911.
On facing page, the front page of Turin's newspaper *La Stampa*, April 30, 1911.

in New York in 1911 and in London in 1914: …a light-hearted view of the middle class, the inhabitants of the slums described in all their primitiveness, the people shrewdly observed in all their merits and defects."

Unlike Vuiller, Crawford Flitch set out to examine the city as an entity made up of houses, streets and urban bustle, but also and above all its human population and their daily lives. "The acute observer will pass underneath the dark archivolts that lead to the quarter of Castello. Here the streets are cut like gullies through solid blocks of foul-smelling, cramped buildings, dark even in the light of an August noon… It is into these long and sunless alleys that Cagliari

and angrily and every family seems to be in the midst of a domestic crisis."

The writer's attitude toward the local bourgeoisie was different, and rich in subtle irony: "It is so refined that it almost persuades you that the middle class of society is still capable of producing some fine flowers of civilization… There is a modest restaurant on the Bastione San Remy, hidden from sight during the day but overflowing into the square with small, white tables in the evening." Crawford Flitch observed the people who went there: "They dress in a gay but unpretentious way, their talk is quiet but animated: something of the dignity and serenity of the evening has seeped into their manners. This bourgeoisie has attained that mode or habit of the spirit by which, it seems to me, you may judge whether a people is truly civilized or not, and that is a calm and delicate seizing of the passing moment, a satisfaction of the body and the mind that can be sustained without the pleasure of the senses or the excitement of external amusements."

Renzo, as an apprentice in his adolescence, learned the rudiments of upholstery in the service of just that middle class so effectively described by Crawford Flitch. In the end, the writer sought to define the charm of the whole of Cagliari as follows: "Every city has the nature of a prison, but none has so many means of escape as Cagliari. With a subtle air of modesty, it denies its allures and continually invites you to look away from it." Tito, Renzo's father, had eleven other children and, convinced that there was no future for them on Sardinian soil, encouraged them to emigrate from an early age. His family would never have been able to attain that "calm and delicate seizing of the passing moment." Tito had never even known that moment, but hoped with all his heart that his children might one day.

For the majority of the inhabitants the economic situation could in fact be compared to those "long and sunless alleys" into which "Cagliari spills its teeming life." Confirmation of this is provided by the travel notes of a little-known writer, Adele Meucci, published at Siena in 1918 under the title *La Sardegna, nelle pagine di uno scrittore inglese*, which refer directly to the author of *Mediterranean Moods*: "I was afraid that Crawford, like so many, had kept aloof from the place… Yet all uncertainty and fear were dispelled in the very first pages and I experienced the deep and intimate joy that comes from finding a spirit in tune with your own in its determination to convey a sincere and enlightened admiration. I wish that people in Italy would come to know Sardinia in the way that people in England must have done through the work of this writer." Certainly this rebuke could not have been addressed to Renzo, who knew his land

Model 127 of 1912.
It is a comfortable, snug form, characterized by the goose-down cushioning that molds the back into plump half-cylinders.

ed il settimo giorno
si riposò sulla ......

POLTRONA
FRAU

Anche a lui

come a ogni mortale — il miglior
ristoro e l'unico riposo (prima di quello
eterno!) — può essere dato da una
delle magnifiche e comode poltrone (in
pelle o imitazione) della Ditta

R. FRAU

in TORINO *(via Palazzo di
Città, N. 6ᵇⁱˢ)*.

Visitare i ma-
gazzeni e chiedere
i cataloghi per
credere!

A witty interpretation of the 127
by Eugenio Colmo, a.k.a. Golia.
Advertising poster and cartoon from
the humorous weekly *Numero*, Turin,
1916.

well and, though loving it, was obliged to seek his own among those "many means of escape," looking far away in the direction of the mainland. "Unlike those who bore his name in ancient Sardinia," writes Daniele Baroni in *Frau. Un nome, una poltrona, una storia*, "he would have nothing to do with the forges of blacksmiths (according to etymology and studies of the origins of surnames, Frau means blacksmith and is a variant of the surname Fabbri, or rather, is a direct derivation of it in the Sardinian dialect)," when he migrated to Turin at that very turning point between the nineteenth and twentieth century that saw, through the psychological sensitivity of Crawford Flitch, "precursor of D.H. Lawrence, author of the insuperable *Sea and Sardinia*, the rediscovery of Sardinia, of an island capable of yielding new emotions and new sensations."

And yet, even if in literature the island managed to escape in those years from the picture painted by the last travelers of the nineteenth century and come to throbbing life in the accounts of their successors, the trials of daily life remained a harsh reality for those who had only their hands to get them through its toil. Tito encouraged Renzo to try his luck on the mainland. "There is little in the records about this young Sardinian," remarks Daniele Baroni. "We know that he moved to Turin… After all Turin still represented the last bastion of an old tie, an emblem of the capital of the former kingdom of Sardinia, even if a culturally remote one." Turin was a lively place, full of attractions. Here the atmosphere was one of endless possibilities. "Apprentice dressmakers, students, scions of the distinguished nobility and the well-to-do bourgeoisie," writes Roberto Antonetto in *Torino l'altro ieri*, "Carnival balls, flirtatious strolls under the porticoes, the elegant crowd at the racecourse, the *bon-ton* places in the center, the *cafés chantants*, the taverns of the suburbs, the magazines filled with thrills and perdition, the well-mannered drawing rooms: a singular blend of Turinese respectability and Parisian-style pleasure-seeking fantasy held sway in the years between the end of the nineteenth century and the Great War. And they were years of an unexpectedly feminine Turin, in which the virility of times gone by seemed to retreat before woman, who had become the center of all that was valuable and enjoyable, from gallant admiration when out strolling to furtive meetings in the private room… the Turinese woman, the working companion and mother of patriots of the past, had never been so feminine, at least as far as she was allowed to be of course. Her elegance became proverbial: lace, flowered hats, ribbons, high-necked blouses, pleated skirts that no longer swelled into a bustle behind; and hat veils, gloves and parasols, to protect pale complexions."

If the sunsets tingeing Monte Santo and the Iglesias chain with purple were still vivid in his memory, the young Renzo was nevertheless fascinated by the bustling pace of life in the Savoy capital, where he found a job as an upholsterer. And, over the course of his brief apprenticeship, he started to observe his urban surroundings, the variegated humanity for whom he did his work. He did his military service in Milan and was discharged with the rank of a lieutenant in the infantry. While there he met Savina Pisati, a girl from Milan whom he married at the end of his service. Savina gave birth to Ugo, their first child, in 1903. However, it was in Turin that Renzo started his own business, in the city whose history went far beyond the tribute paid to it by Guido Gozzano (1883–1916) in his *Elogio*, verging on nostalgia for a past that had vanished forever. "A bit old-fashioned, provincial, green / but with such a Parisian charm, / in you I become a child again, / I find my youthful grace / and you are as dear to me as / the serving wench who watched my birth, o Turin. / You saw my birth, indulged / the dreams of the boy lost in reverie: / all of myself, all my past, / my most tender and wistful memories / sleep in you, buried like clothes / buried amid camphor in a closet." And then the pavilion that the city prepared for the Exposition of 1911, the year of publication of his *Colloqui*, caused the poet to exclaim: "Blessed are the old who were young in those memorable years." As Roberto Antonetto points out: "At bottom, Gozzano's ironic enchantment with the petty sentiments of his contemporaries can be seen as regret for something momentous from the past that cannot be brought back to life… The new Turin is another place, finding its new glories in the enterprise of its businessmen, and in the conquests of the working class. The two things that were to most thoroughly revolutionize twentieth-century life, cinema and the automobile, were born in Turin." And so we have the different bourgeoisies: static, clinging on to privilege, that of Cagliari; ready to seize the moment, in full and pulsating transformation, that of Turin. It was to the latter that Renzo now offered his services. And the young man did not lack the necessary enterprise. All he had to do was make the best of the flair he already had, in the city which on July 1, 1899, marked the beginning of the history of the automobile in Italy, with that deed under the seal of a notary declaring the establishment of Fiat and "bearing the signatures of a group of pioneers, including Giovanni

A. Bonzagni, *Coming out of La Scala*, 1910. Milan, Civica Galleria d'Arte Moderna.
Poster by Marcello Dudovich, *circa* 1913. Treviso, Museo Civico Luigi Bailo, collezione Salce.

Agnelli," as Antonetto tells us. "The first plant was a small one: 10,000 square meters, on Corso Dante, at numbers 35–37, with fifty employees. Its output in 1900, which was in a way Fiat's 'year zero': twenty-four vehicles. The first of the Fiat 31/2 hp models roared through the dismayed streets of Turin. Six years later the plant was five times bigger, with 2500 employees and output had risen to 1149 cars. In 1907, Fiat won the three most important races in the world: the Targa Florio, the Grand Prix of the Automobile Club de France, and the Kaiser's Cup in Germany… Between 1905 and 1907, the years when the economic boom of the Giolitti era reached its peak, there were seventy automobile manufacturers in Italy: twenty of them were in Turin, many others in Piedmont. Then there were six body builders, the RIV, six tire makers, three head-light manufacturers, two chassis work-shops, one factory producing fuel tanks, another magnetos, yet another brakes and three making accessories."

Renzo was still the attentive observer that he had shown

17

Model 96 of 1915, the armchair most frequently portrayed in the advertisements carried by *Numero* of Turin, has a back divided up into a geometric pattern by straps.

himself to be right from his first apprenticeship and the world of automobiles and the allied activities that were continually springing up gave him ideas for new areas of enterprise: demanding customers commissioned their cars from renowned body builders, just like suits from the tailor, and the interiors of these vehicles required the services of the best saddlers and upholsterers. In addition, the cinema offered real opportunities: the creation of sets, however temporary, for the movies that were being made entailed the supply of furnishings, and for the most part these consisted of drapes and upholstered furniture. In fact armchairs and couches

movie making into a significant player on the international scene and within just a few years turning his production company into a feared rival of such famous names as Gaumont, Pathé, Kalem, Triangle, First National, Metro, Hollandia, Nordisk and Svenska." Thus Turin quickly became the film capital of Italy: silent films, of course, as sound did not make its appearance until the thirties.

By 1903, the year when Renzo Frau's first child was born, "Arturo Ambrosio," according to Roberto Antonetto, "was already a movie producer in the modern sense, and was turning out title after title, from drama to comedy to docu-

Il Rosario della colpa, silent film by Mario Almirante, 1920; on the set, the 96 armchair. Turin, Museo Nazionale del Cinema.

were often in the foreground of such scenes. Renzo was convinced that the automobile and the movie were good news for his trade.

"The number of spectators was growing," explains Gigi Caorsi in *Torino città viva da capitale a metropoli 1880–1980*, "new movie theaters were opening all over Italy: aggressive foreign production companies, first from France and then America, Germany and Scandinavia, fought with no holds barred for a share in such a promising market. And it was at this point that the Turinese Arturo Ambrosio came to the fore, transforming the humble Italian cottage industry of

mentary (the Susa-Moncenisio automobile race and then the earthquake in Messina filmed by the cameraman Roberto Omegna). *The Last Days of Pompeii* of 1902, *Quo Vadis* of 1912, *Ashes* of 1916 (Eleonora Duse's only film), movies which have gone down in legend, were all Ambrosio Film productions. In 1908, the director of the equally celebrated Itala Film was Giovanni Pastrone, often working under the pseudonym of Piero Fosco, who took Italian cinema to new heights with *Cabiria*. The first screening of *Cabiria*, in 1914, was a great event for Turin. The drama, coscripted by Gabriele D'Annunzio and with music by

Ildebrando Pizzetti, was shown at the Teatro Vittorio Emanuele, with a hundred and fifty members of the Orchestra and Choir of the Regio performing the music in the auditorium. The stars were Italia Almirante Manzini, Umberto Mozzato and Maciste. On the eve of the twenties, before it went into decline, cinematography was the third biggest industry in Italy and about half of the around a hundred studios were based in Turin. Their films were bought sight unseen on foreign markets."

D'Annunzio himself spoke of his encounter with Pastrone in his *Del Cinematografo considerato come strumento di liberazione e come arte di trasfigurazione*, published in 1914, lamenting the level of production at the time: "The taste of the public has reduced cinematography today to a more or less vulgar industry in competition with the theater. I myself, in order to get hold of that famous red meat which is needed to inflame the courage of my running dogs, have allowed some of my best-known plays to be mangled into movies. But this time (oh what dishonor! Unbelievable ignominy!) I was tempted to get directly involved. A Turinese studio, run by a cultured and energetic man who has an extraordinary feel for the medi-

La poltrona dei Signori !!!!
I Signori della poltrona !!!!

um, produced an example of popular art based on an unpublished treatment that I provided. It was the outline of a historical novel, jotted down many years ago and found among my innumerable papers… The studio has, without doubt, made the greatest and most daring effort ever attempted in this art. It consists of grand historical vignettes linked together by an adventure story that caters to the most ingenuous popular sentiment. And my beloved Ildebrando from Parma has composed a wonderful symphonic poem for *Cabiria*, a 'Symphony of Fire' redder and more crackling than the glitter of the Valkyries."

Thus D'Annunzio assigned to Giovanni Pastrone, whom he referred to by his pseudonym of Piero Fosco, and his Turinese studio an absolute supremacy, to which even his favorite composer Ildebrando Pizzetti of Parma had contributed. So Renzo was surrounded by a wide range of ferments in Turin during those early years of the twentieth century: "Both of them young, the same age, automobile and cinema walked arm in arm." Actors and actresses, good and bad, vied to attract attention, giving rise to the completely new phenomenon of the star system.

At the age of just nineteen, Pinin Farina was in charge of design at his brother Giovanni's body shop and had earned the trust and respect of Giovanni Agnelli, and the friendship of Vincenzo Lancia. "Foreign actresses and actors came to Turin, like the famous American Leslie Carter who liked Turinese automobiles, as did her compatriot Revelle Hamilton. Leslie Carter," Pinin Farina told Ernesto Caballo, who has collected his memories in *Pininfarina. Nato con l'automobile*, "arrived with fifty trunks and seven greyhounds on a leash. Some actresses did not just visit the dressmakers' workshops—there were some well-known names, Bellom, Trinelli, Gori—but also turned up with their escorts at the body shops. Maria Jacobini, Pina Menichelli and Italia Almirante Manzini were vamps, as was Lyda Borelli, the star of *Amor mio non muore*… Once Lyda got into an Isotta Fraschini that we

Model 96 in the artwork of Properzi
from the Frau catalogue and three
postcards from the twenties.

Poster for Giovanni Pastrone's movie *Cabiria*, 1914, based on a script by Gabriele d'Annunzio.
Poster for the movie *Za la mort* starring Emilio Ghione, 1915. Turin, Museo Nazionale del Cinema.

had just finished and it looked as if it were made just for the actress and for her beauty … Quite a few actors turned up along with these film stars, Alberto Collo, Mario Bonnard, Alberto Capozzi: inevitably they too carried their acting over into real life... The producers Arturo Ambrosio and Ernesto Pasquali—and he was a director as well—were good customers… They had some skilled cameramen like Vitrotti, Omegna, who was Guido Gozzano's cousin and made the documentary *La Vita delle farfalle* with him, Scalenghe and Chiusano. They filmed quite a few beauty contests for the cars, to which actresses were invited to launch the new models. It was almost a tradition: as far back as 1900, the Fiat 3 1/2 hp had had Tina di Lorenzo on board for its inaugural run along the avenues of the Valentino… Pasquali introduced me to, among others, Nino Oxilia and Sandro Camasio who had also started to direct movies. And through him I got to know Giovanni Pastrone, someone who didn't talk much. It was said that he was working on new processes and systems for cinematography."

For *Cabiria*, in fact, Pastrone was to develop a system that allowed the camera to be moved around and thus permitted variation in the depth of field. But the most popular of the stars who frequented the body shops of Turin was unquestionably Emilio Ghione, known as Za la Mort after the most

famous of his characters. Gigi Caorsi says of him: "In the years of his greatest success, around 1915, Ghione was earning as much as a hundred thousand lire a month." He could certainly afford the finest automobiles, even if "he could lose seventy thousand in a single hand of poker without batting an eyelid," as G.C. Castello recalls in his book, where he also mentions the star's caprices, no less celebrated than those of the actress Francesca Bertini: "he used to sign contracts and then break them, start work on movies and leave them halfway through, continually getting involved in legal disputes."

Yet his personality so stirred people's imagination that "rummaging through the sack of placated but not forgotten childhood terrors, we understand the reaction of the waiter who, as G.G. Napolitano recounts in his beautiful *Omaggio a Ghione*, given the job of taking orders from the journalist and actor, approached the table at which they were seated trembling with fear. It was Za la Mort he was afraid of, having seen the movie as a child and believed in it totally. As for Ghione, he was the Turinese hooligan of the 'Gray Rats,' dressed in velvet, with his pants tied at the ankles, capable of the worst kind of violence." And Za la Mort quickly joined the ranks of popular legend. "While Paris grew dark / under the pale moon," runs one of the old recordings selected and presented by Pasquito del Bosco in *Fonografo italiano 1890-1940*, "far from the madding crowd / Za la Mort keeps vigil; / he is the deadly apache / everyone believes him brutal / while his heart is true / he knows no egoism and cowardice! / Za la Mort / knight of mystery! / Za la Mort / with the eyes of a warrior! / It is true that you steal / but the shady spoils are not for you, / but just for your sad companions / of the streets!"

So the automobile and cinema were really going hand in

POLTRONA **FRAU**

AMMINISTR. E FABBRICA:
VIA MODENA, 33
TELEFONO 22-160
TORINO

ESIGETE SEMPRE LA VERA
POLTRONA **FRAU**
CHE PORTA IMPRESSO A
FUOCO NEI FIANCHI IL
MARCHIO DI FABBRICA

ESPOSIZIONE:
VIA S. TERESA, 13
TELEFONO 42-368

*Poltrona tipo " Lira „
con cuscino velluto*

The Lira armchair, 1916,
in an advertisement from the time:
decidedly frivolous
in its feminine form.

hand through the streets of the city when, in 1912, Renzo registered his name—a name whose roots went all the way back to Vulcan's forge—on the roll of artisans at the Turin Chamber of Commerce, in the category of upholsterers, and really got his business going. The first hard years were over, years when he could only count on the help of the Sardinian community, for there were many of his fellow islanders living in the shade of the Mole Antonelliana. Now he had a craft, and was already experimenting with the various possibilities offered by the many activities that were thriving in Turin around the two main industries: automobile manufacturing and the cinema. "Alongside Alessio," recalls Pinin Farina in *Nato con l'automobile*, "there were Locati and Torretta, Ciocca, Lanza, Schieppati, Conte and Gossetti, Taurus, Christillin, Conrotto; then, with my brother, others were added, Rossi and Bussolotti, Schenone, Tondini, Viarengo and Filipponi, Olitano and more." And the number of constructors was growing: "As well as Fiat, there were already Ceirano, Itala, Scat, Spà, Turin which later became Diatto, Fides and Fert. Another make, Aquila, had its plant on the Po although this, unlike the Dora, was not an 'industrial' river. It could be said that a new one sprang up every season: Otav, Lux, Star, Tre Spade at the Bertoldo Foundries on the border with Nice."

Among the body builders who made use of Renzo's services was Pinin Farina, right from the time when he used to work in his brother Giovanni's shop, and among the constructors, Vincenzo Lancia. Frau armchairs, on the other hand, were unmistakable presences on the sets of the movie studios in Turin, and even in Rome, when Turin's star began to wane. However, Renzo had been planning his moves for years. As well as working as an upholsterer, in fact, he was the representative for G. Gribaudi, manager of the Turin branch of the Monza importer Paolo Meda di

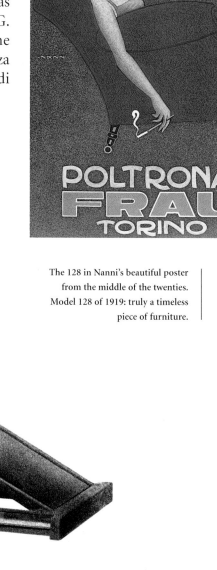

The 128 in Nanni's beautiful poster
from the middle of the twenties.
Model 128 of 1919: truly a timeless
piece of furniture.

Bernardo, for sales of a product invented in England, an imitation leather known as leatherette and sold in Italy under the name "Dermoide." For a long time Dermoide was the only product sold by Gribaudi, but when he went into retirement, in 1909, Renzo took over the management of the branch, with its offices at Via Palazzo di Città, no. 6 bis, and started to sell hides, braid and all the other varied requirements of upholsterers. This gave him the opportunity to familiarize himself with the production of his customers and competitors. He went to France, Germany and Austria to get hold of products of superior quality to the ones available on the domestic market. Both these activities, upholstery and the sale of materials, soon proved sources of undoubted satisfaction.

Fashion photograph published in *Vogue America*, 1919; in the same year Giovanni Caproni designed the CA 60 flying boat.

In those years Renzo was even rewarded for the volume of business he had attained with Dermoide by a journey to England. For some time he had been thinking about becoming an entrepreneur, but he did not want his products to be identified with the eclecticism of a clearly French character that distinguished the line of upholstered furniture produced by workshops in Turin, by those customers and rivals of his who, in response to the demand from the newest members of the bourgeoisie, were modifying and adapting tried and tested forms. Nor was he attracted by the art nouveau style, with which he had been familiar ever since the Exposition of Decorative Arts held in Turin in 1902. This had presented furniture, articles of everyday use, decoration, graphics and even architecture: the pavilions were designed by Raimondo D'Aronco. In the same year, Giacomo Cometti, one of the greatest exponents of Turinese and Italian modernism, was awarded a diploma of honor at the exposition and opened his own workshop in the city.

"It was the Turin of the period between the two international expositions of 1898 and 1911," writes Giovanni Tesio in *Torino città viva da capitale a metropoli 1880-1980*, "with the

1919

Archivio Frau

Model 1919, replica of the 128 armchair. A decidedly rare example of a prototype and, at the same time, summation of the upholstered armchair: this is how it was described by the weekly *L'Espresso* on March 4, 1979.

city's old carriages and, already, the first motor cabs; with the excitement of the first conveyor belts at the local fairs and the equal excitement of the first general strike in 1904, poised between the Piedmontese dialect and the Italian language: a beautiful city—a city of a bold and composed beauty and full of promise. Zino Zini has written about it with restrained nostalgia. First of all he describes its physical attributes: 'the circle of the Alps, incomparable in its majestic solemnity,' 'the undulating and somewhat languid line of the wooded hills,' the river Po, 'the network of symmetrical streets and squares,' 'superb and endless lines of avenues, not to be found anywhere else in the world, sprouting the first leaves in March and turning into true rivers of copper yellow in October dusks, and then, skeletal and bare in the winter, decked out with frost and snow.'"

Here, the automobile was still caught in the spell of the "restrained nostalgia" that distinguishes the writer Zino Zini's portrait of the city. In reality, however, it heralded the imminent disruption of the urban and natural scenery, as the horse-drawn vehicle went into inexorable decline and was replaced by the motor vehicle. The whole of the industry of progress conspired with the automobile to radically alter the landscape. The form of the automobile was to reject any affinity with the carriage. This was due not just to the brilliance of its designers but also to the need of constructors to give a suitable image to the most fascinating of the products of technology, to allow its mechanical function to find the best way to express itself. And it was also a consequence of the serial process of construction.

An acute observer of the industrial scene in Turin, thanks to his links with body builders and automobile constructors, Renzo realized that furniture, on the contrary, ran the risk of no longer responding to its function and often, especially where upholstered seats were concerned, of losing itself in pure decoration. There was no easy way out of this, for someone who was born to the craft and knew its limitations. Renzo knew of one, unique case: Michael Thonet had invent-ed a system of construction that overcame the limits of artisan production at a bound and introduced the techniques of mass production into the furniture sector. Yet he was not so much interested in the system itself as in the fact that Thonet had really managed to give a new form to the chair: his models were out of the ordinary run. The automobile was a quite different case: it did not develop out of the carriage and its form was an immediate expression of the mechanism. Even before the age of the mechanical horse had begun, however, as Karl Mang points out in his *The History of Modern Furniture*, "in 1819 Michael Thonet (1796–1871) opened a carpentry shop at Boppard on the Rhine and, around 1830, began to experiment with bending wood to make the individual parts of furniture in the Biedermeier style. He tried this out first with the headrests and backs of chairs: covered with a thick layer of veneer, these were glued and pressed in a wooden form. As time went by he found solutions to ever more difficult problems and, as he perfected the technique, simplified the forms and lightened the structure. The elegant and lightweight chairs that he designed around 1840 proved such a success that Prince Metternich persuaded Michael Thonet to move to Vienna and ensured his economic security by obtaining him commissions from wealthy noble houses. For the Liechtenstein Palace in Vienna, which was completed in those very years (1843–46), he designed chairs whose gracefulness and purity of form earns them a place among the finest examples of nineteenth-century furniture... With the construction of his first factory at Koritschan (Moravia),

Michael Thonet showed himself to be a true pioneer of the new industry: he designed the building himself, oversaw its construction and fitting out and, together with his five sons, built most of the machinery."

With his technique of steam bending copper-beech wood, Michael Thonet invented a system for the mass production of a piece of furniture, the chair, that had always been made by hand. In developing the technical process of construction, he succeeded in reconciling the form and function of the object itself. But Thonet's chair was an industrial product and all the other, hand-built types of furniture on sale were expressions of different local versions of the prevailing eclectic style. No easy way out presented itself to Renzo, who was determined to found his business on the knowledge of the craft.

an old script that confined such variation to decoration. It had to be treated as an object in its own right, as it is the one that best meets the need of every age. Only in this way would it be accepted as a discreet and unmistakable presence among all those other pieces of furniture, in all their variety. On the other hand the armchair performs the function that makes it useful as much as any seat does, but not in the same way. The armchair is the fruit of a reappraisal of the form of the seat, and hence a design. Consequently, in intention at least, it fulfills the function better. Good or bad, all chairs are the same, except for the armchair which, by definition, is a comfortable seat, subject to an assessment of quality on the part of its user: for this reason it is described as more comfortable, less comfortable, even uncomfortable, always in

Model 1919 in the total harmony of its form; details showing the side and the extreme softness of the seat.

Nevertheless, he chose to set himself apart from the crowd, by restoring upholstered furniture to its function and seeking to find the shape that best fulfilled its potential. He concentrated on a single form, the armchair, making use of the most tried and tested craft techniques, the only ones he knew and was capable of applying, but seeking to perfect them and overcome their limits. So, if Giacinto Carena (1778–1859), in his *Prontuario di vocaboli attenenti a parecchie arti, ad alcuni mestieri, a cose domestiche, e altre di uso comune* written almost sixty years earlier, had already defined the function of the armchair as "made to provide a more comfortable seat for better repose and even for sleeping in," there was no reason to confound this with the delirious range of rehashes of

comparison with another, but not with just any chair, for it is, *par excellence*, the chair. However, only the design capable of making the reality correspond to the appearance will be able to guarantee the harmony of the product: and so the armchair that appears to be comfortable, really is.

And the armchairs and couches must have looked comfortable to that German official who, "sent to Edwardian England to examine the state of architecture there," comments Daniele Baroni, "rediscovered and brought back to the Continent the intrinsic values of the English home, the simple criteria on which it was based, the pleasure of a mellow, unostentatious sense of well-being, the decency of a private life spent around the fireplace."

Bottle of Chanel No. 5 perfume, launched in 1921 by the famous Parisian fashion house. Model 22 of 1922: a comfortable armchair, though designed for a more erect, less slumped posture: decidedly for conversation, not repose.

The Prussian Hermann Muthesius (1861–1927), was one of the founders, in 1907, of the Deutscher Werkbund, which brought together artists, architects, craftsmen and manufacturers in an attempt to establish a collaboration between the worlds of art and industry. In 1896 he had been sent to London as cultural attaché to the German embassy, with the express task of studying British architecture and applied arts. On his return, he published *Das Englische Haus*, a work in three volumes that came out between 1904 and 1908 and had a great success in Europe.

Renzo had already encountered furniture in Austria and Germany that neither imitated the styles of the past nor adopted those in fashion. Yet the ones made in Great Britain were really something different, especially when compared with the range of furniture produced in the rest of Europe. And this was particularly true of the armchairs, which were comfortable even if a bit ungainly and perhaps too opulent. So he decided to use the trip across the Channel that he been awarded for his work with Dermoide to test these convictions. His plan was to take those models and perfect them, to subject them to a sort of purifying *maquillage*: a choice, therefore, that in limiting the range of products, would place the emphasis on excellence of construction and quality of materials. And his armchairs would to all intents and purposes be the result of that choice: timeless furniture.

"In 1926," observes Franco Moschini, "the famous cartoonist Eugenio Colmo, known as Golia, even portrayed the Eternal Father seated on the 127 of 1912, resting from the labor of Creation. He chose that armchair because it was visibly soft and in his view the best suited to ensuring the King of Heaven's repose. But his choice confirmed, even then, that the chair was not linked to a particular time, in the sense of fashion or custom. I realized myself, when I was trying to reconstruct the history of Frau production in the sixties, that the original models, however threadbare and shabby, did not look like old furniture. It seemed natural to describe them as classics. That's why I thought it was a good idea to produce replicas of them."

In 1912, in order to put his plans into practice, Renzo set up the administrative and commercial offices of his business in premises on Via Palazzo di Città, right in the center of town and close to Piazza San Carlo. He then rented some old stables at no. 33, Via Modena, on the outskirts of the city in those days, and converted them into a factory. His next step was to get hold of the best workforce available, and the advertisement printed on the poster left no room for misun-

31

Armchair 177 of 1925 and couch 577:
first fruit of Renzo's decision
to produce coordinated suites
of furniture. The couch matches
the armchair in the perfect rigor
of its form.
Letter from Soleri to Renzo Frau, 1925.
On facing page, the 177
in an advertising postcard designed
by Mendez in the twenties.

Poltrona 177 senza cuscino

Dolce riposo inebria
sulle soffici piume…
della Poltrona Frau.

Esigete sempre la vera Poltrona FRAU
che porta impresso a fuoco nei fianchi
il marchio di Fabbrica.

derstandings: "Wanted: highly skilled upholsterer. Apply to the firm R. Frau, Via Palazzo di Città 6 bis." Putting it in the singular, upholsterer, reinforced the nature of the specification: the highly skilled, as Renzo was well aware, were rare. Craftsmen from workshops and saddlers from the automobile body shops responded to the advertisement. Renzo hired fourteen of the best applicants, along with four women who were expert sewers of leather.

His definition of upholstered furniture entailed the choice of a material that provided the best finish. And what could that be? Leather, and only leather, the most extreme and unchallenged of materials: sought-after and displayed since ancient times, flayed from the animal, leather becomes soft to the touch after tanning, a gentle, seductive caress. And the origins of treatment to which it is subjected before use are lost in the mists of time. In discourse LXXXV of his *Piazza universale di tutte le professioni del mondo*, Tommaso Garzoni da Bagnocavallo (1549–1589) wrote: "Called by the Romans *alutarii*: whence even Plautus in one of his comedies called a master leather maker *alutarius Cerdo*; known by the more familiar term of *coriarius*, and in Italian *cuoiaio*, who by the Spaniard is called *cortidor que adoba cueros*… Their materials and tools are hides, lime and valonia, or oak bark or box, and flaying knives; and then the hides are put to soak, and in the lime, and flayed, and then suitably dressed." And in the notes to discourse LXXXV: "Of the leather makers Garimberto said that they were brothers of the bow maker, because the bow maker pulls the bowstring so hard that sometime he breaks it, and the leather maker pulls the leather so hard that sometimes he tears it with his teeth." In discourse LXXXI he discusses the craftsman who used to serve the horse and its rider: "We find the saddler with his tools, strings, lime screen, hide, cords and rods to beat the hide, out of which he makes the saddles and measures them. In which we note the parts, and the styles of saddle, that is the stock, … pommel, …and saddlecloth. And then the straps, …stirrup leathers, breast strap, crupper strap, crupper, …and slings; and likewise the halter, the bridle with its parts and styles, that is the reins, and their button, the headstall, the throatlatch, with the types of saddles and bridles: Roman, 'alla ginetta', French, English, German, Turkish and others."

The craft has always involved anatomical study of both the man and the animal: the former rides well when the horse is saddled well. This is why Renzo showed a preference for saddlers rather than for other craftsmen: his customers would be well mounted if the armchairs were well-made saddles. Of course an experienced foreman was needed, and Renzo chose for the role an upholsterer who had been trained in Paris and who had learned techniques that were completely unknown in Turin, such as ways of padding the arms and sides: at that time the French were the undisputed masters of upholstered furniture. At his side he placed an excellent cutter of hides. To ensure that he got the best workers available he decided to pay them slightly higher wages than the going rate and thereby roused the ire of those of his competitors who would not even have dreamed of doing so. He also adopted the British custom of giving them Saturday off and assigned an assistant to each of his workers.

Then he started developing the models, subjecting them to a process of purification aimed at the definition of a better thought-out range of merchandise. "Comparing his products," comments Daniele Baroni, "with those available abroad leads to some interesting conclusions. Even the renowned 'sense of proportion' of the most famous English cabinetmakers was taken further. The padding was reduced, all opulent forms eliminated and decoration banished. Only the working of the leather served to shape and model the piece, leaving the stuffing soft, its curves followed by regular and rhythmic pleats, containing and puffing it up with the quilting, bringing it out with borders and straps. In this way the form 'justified' itself, every slight modification of the surface made sense and thus the armchair was molded like a body, stimulating its tactile qualities to a point verging on sensuality." If the form "justified itself, stimulating its tactile qualities to a point verging on sensuality," then the armchair summed up all the distinctive features of the function of upholstered furniture.

As for the couch, Renzo was well aware that its extended form required simplification. And not through any difference in the care taken over its upholstering or in the quality of the materials used: simplification here meant form, derived and therefore extended. In Renzo's view the couch was a consequence of the armchair: first the armchair, then the couch, and never the other way round in the order of aesthetic definition. This explains the absolute insistence on the logo: "The Frau armchair must always be branded on the sides with the trademark that guarantees its origin." So the trademark (Poltrona Frau) was applied to the molded body and by extension to its derived form, the couch. And the branding was also a confirmation, according to Renzo, of the only possible material for the best definition of the object: leather.

"The solution," explains Franco Moschini, "was certainly an improvement on that of the label: the competition had no hesitation in forging the latter and Renzo rightly considered the faking of an indelible mark a more difficult and risky undertaking." At the time he was responsible for the promotion of his products and had to guarantee them in every way, given the existence of a distribution network that by now covered the whole of the country.

"Even during the years of the Great War," notes Daniele Baroni, "the first advertisements for his company started to appear in journals that had an interregional circulation (*Numero* of Turin, in 1915), wittily illustrated by his artist friends, including Golia (the lawyer Eugenio Colmo), a famous satirical cartoonist and commercial artist from Turin who was one of the leading figures at the independent humorous weekly." On July 18, 1915, the editorial staff of *Numero* greeted with joy Colmo's marriage to Lia Tregnaghi, also from Turin: "In these days our dear Golia has completed a design, his best and most successful ever: the design... of entwining his destiny with that of a cultured and very charming young lady. From these columns of his and our own we send him, to the sweet refuge of these days, our most heartfelt, most cordial good wishes." Golia was later to draw the famous cartoon of Emperor Franz Joseph comfortably seated on the Frau Armchair 127, before going to his eternal repose. And then, having seated the potentates of the earth, the cartoonist could not leave out God, resting from the labors of Creation.

Meanwhile Renzo, in the early twenties, "set out to improve the image of the catalogue as well, with a fine publication illustrated with stereotypes and printed in two colors..." A total of twenty-three different models of armchair were presented in this catalogue, many of them in suites of furniture that included a couch. All the models were shown with leather coverings, which in line with the tanning methods and technology available at the time consisted of sheepskin, Morocco leather and cowhide... Of the tendencies of the

Renzo Frau's armchairs on movie sets at the end of the twenties: Carlo Aldini's *Uomo in frak*; Gennaro Righelli's *Der Präsident*; Guido Brignone's *Le retour*; Mario Camerini Fert-Pittaluga's *La casa dei pulcini*. Turin, Museo Nazionale del Cinema.

early part of the century, such as art nouveau, there was not the slightest trace in those models. And yet among Frau's competitors there were firms like those of Eugenio Quarti in Milan or Ducrot in Palermo, both heavily engaged on the front of the new style."

Eugenio Colmo and other friends suggested to Renzo ironic variations on the infinite merits of his armchairs, which appeared in the adverts published in *Numero*. "These are Sad Times! Do you want health???? Peace????? Good cheer??? Strength???? Tranquility? Recline in a comfortable armchair made by the R. Frau firm, Via Palazzo di Città no. 6 bis, Turin. To be convinced just visit our warehouses and ask for the catalogue." At that time only the best-organized manufacturers produced catalogues, and Renzo was determined that his should be one of them. "In his advertising," confirms Daniele Baroni, "he concentrated above all on associating Poltrona Frau with the concept of 'superlative...' Toward the end of the twenties, even though Renzo played no active part in the more avant-garde circles of the city's culture, Frau's armchairs—along with Lenci's *bisquits*—could be considered to lie at the heart of the activities of some of the protagonists of Turinese *Novecentismo*, such as Gigi Chessa and Umberto Cuzzi, or Casorati himself at Palazzo Gualino; in other words, the cultural sphere of the artists with closest ties to the most vital centers in Europe at the time, the Vienna of Hoffmann and Dagobert Peche and the Munich of Bruno Paul."

Renzo had seen the armchair as an object with no relation to current fashions or daring innovations and had restored it to its true function through a process of purification aimed at bringing balance back to its configuration. Renzo's armchair was a form "made to provide a more comfortable seat for better repose and even for sleeping in," but did not fit the now outdated definition of Giacinto Carena, "the name used today for an ample stuffed seat, provided with cushions." Nor could it be confused with the other pieces that made up the varied range of furniture. Poltrona Frau was to all intents and purposes the armchair and within a few years its fame had spread all over the country.

Unlike Thonet who, in his time, had invented an industrial system of construction capable of producing a chair that reconciled technology and aesthetics, Renzo drew on existing models of upholstered furniture and therefore retained their artisan system of construction, unwilling to risk losing their meaning by improving on this system. For this reason he delegated the construction of the frames to specialized workshops, as he had no workers capable of carrying out this task. He knew very well that the sturdiness, and thus the durability, of his armchairs and couches depended in part on the seasoning of the wood and the perfect structure of the frame. Highly skilled workers of this kind were already operating in Turin, the men who made the masks used by the panel beaters who constructed bodies for automobiles. It was to them that Renzo turned to get the best. Onto those perfect frames

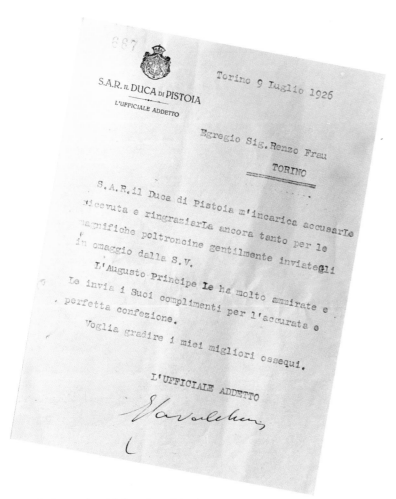

As these testimonials from the period show, Renzo Frau's armchairs found their way into the homes of the aristocracy.

his workers attached hemp straps and steel springs, in the shape of upside-down truncated cones, and then sewed them together with hemp thread, covered them with waste and then jute canvas and placed a layer of horsehair on top. It was through these totally artisan methods of construction that the product was brought to the finishing stage, ready to be upholstered and fitted with goose-down cushions. The finished objects could only be distinguished by the color of the leather—brown, dark red, dark brown and black—and never by different modes of construction. And leather couches and armchairs were soon to become status symbols, marks of an exclusive and leisured lifestyle.

"In the hall, Leo took off his hat and coat," wrote Alberto Moravia (1907–1990) in *Gli Indifferenti* (*The Time of Indifference*), "and helped Carla remove her raincoat. The hall was spacious and white, with three doors opening onto it. Opposite the entrance there was a large dark and rectangular window that undoubtedly gave onto an inner courtyard. They went into the drawing room. 'Let's sit here,' said Leo, pointing at a large leather couch covered with cushions. They sat down: a lamp with a red shade set on a small table illuminated them to breast height. Their heads and the rest of the room remained in semidarkness. For a moment they remained motionless and did not speak: Carla looked around without curiosity. Her gaze strayed from the bottle of liqueur on the table to the walls. Rather than looking at anything, she seemed to be waiting anxiously for a word or a gesture. Leo contemplated Carla. 'So, my dear,' he said at last, 'what's the matter? Why won't you speak or even look at me? Come on, tell me what you're thinking, and if you want something don't be shy. Ask for whatever you want, just as if you were at home.' He reached out and caressed the girl's serious face with his fingers."

If leather couches and armchairs were to be found in the drawing rooms of the wealthy middle class, first-class passengers on the transatlantic liners did not want to do without the comforts they were accustomed to on dry land. "Verne came from the progressive stock of the bourgeoisie: his work serves to show that nothing can escape humanity's grasp," wrote Roland Barthes (1915–80), in *Mythologies*. "So what Jules Verne is doing at bottom is, incontestably, appropriation. The image of the boat, so important in Verne's mythology, does not contradict this at all. On the contrary, the boat can of course be a symbol of departure; more profoundly, it is a code for enclosure. The pleasure we find in the ship is always that of being perfectly enclosed, of keeping the maximum number of objects within reach and of having access to an absolutely infinite space: loving ships means, first of all, loving a superb house, as it is completely enclosed, and not at all grand departures for the unknown: the ship is a type of habitation before it is a means of transport."

And it is to "a superb house" that Pierluigi Cerri referred, when he declared to the writer in *Intervista*, November 1997, that: "Ships are measured in millimeters. Construction is therefore a process of absolute caliber." A well-known architect and designer, Cerri has designed some of the most beautiful ships that ply the seas today. "Everything is justified and requires justification. There are problems of weight, of new materials, of plant engineering. Le Corbusier invited architects to learn from naval engineers. Then between the wars, shipbuilding reached very high levels of sophistication." And on the subject of design today, "the shipbuilder provides the guidelines for the hull, the disposition of spaces and their interaction, what is known as naval planning. These limitations cannot be ignored: they constitute the outline, the framework, from which, along with the technical ones, you set out to construct the inner shell. And there are two quite distinct ways of proceeding. The recent American one takes no notice of the shell of the ship and creates another one,

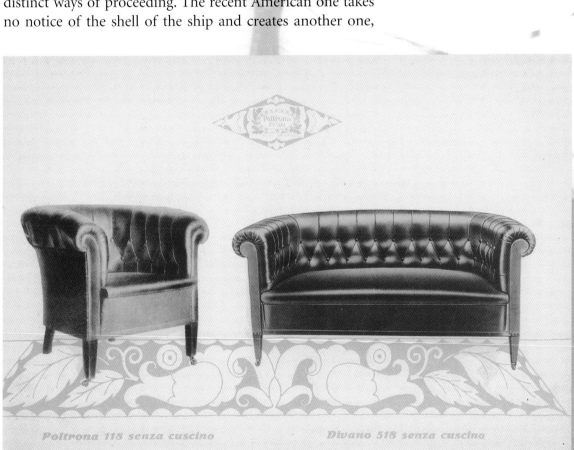

Poltrona 118 senza cuscino   Divano 518 senza cuscino

Armchair 118 and couch 518 of 1929. The model entered production when Savina Pisati assumed control of the company after Renzo's death. In the background, the woman of the twenties in Santa Proud's portrait of a model, 1928.

Fumoir armchairs and couches,
replicas of model 118 of 1929, on the
stage of the roof garden of the Grande
Albergo Vesuvio in Naples, dedicated
to Enrico Caruso.

inside it, that is completely unconnected. These are the Disneyland sort of ships. I try to take the European approach, the one that puts the ship first. It plows the sea, sees the sea. So I try to keep the design of the outer and the inner shell as close as possible. On board a ship you should find and breathe a naval atmosphere, with all the cultural weight of the shipbuilding tradition."

"Between the wars," asserts Pierluigi Cerri, "shipbuilding reached very high levels of sophistication." And, by fortunate coincidence, Poltrona Frau contributed to the fitting out of those ships, at a time when the firm's workers were able to meet the production schedule involved. While the average output of a worker was initially one perfectly finished armchair every three days, the times were progressively reduced, reaching, under exceptional circumstances, the record rate of one armchair a day.

In addition to paying higher wages than were customary for the category, Renzo even offered bonuses for individuals who could work more rapidly, as long as this was not at the expense of quality. Owing to their strong competitive spirit and dedication, the workers at Poltrona Frau soon came to be regarded as master craftsmen and youths vied to be taken on as their apprentices. It was against this background that Renzo was presented with the Ducrot opportunity.

"In Palermo, a city with a great artistic tradition but certain-ly not an industrial one," writes Daniele Baroni in *Bello quotidiano*, "a factory of furniture and applied arts, run by Vittorio Ducrot, had earned a high international reputation and attained a scale that would hardly ever be equaled by other companies subsequently... Since 1899 the company was involved in the realization of one of the most significant works of Italian art nouveau, the furnishings of the Grand Hotel Villa Igieia in Palermo, to designs by Ernesto Basile... In the sector of major contracts, the company had specialized in the field of furnishings and decorations for theaters, cafés, hotels, stores, steamers and transatlantic liners. Ducrot had produced the furnishings of the Hotel de Milan and the Excelsior in Venice, as well as the Teatro Massimo in Palermo." Ducrot had departments specializing in the design and production of custom-made furniture. However, it was in need of contributions to its production potential from outside where the more exclusive settings were concerned. It was official supplier to Ciga, Florio, the Compagnia Italiana di Navigazione, Lloyd Sabaudo and Lloyd Triestino. So the company proposed that Poltrona Frau, already known for the

The Fumoir armchair and couch, replicas of the 118 of 1929, timeless furniture in time.

41

quality of its products, should collaborate on the supply of first-rate upholstered furniture. Renzo accepted readily and this marked the beginning of a period that was highly propitious to the growth of Poltrona Frau, and one that extended well beyond the all too short lifetime of its founder, since the link with Ducrot was maintained right through the thirties. Thus Frau armchairs and couches were the mark of distinction, of exclusivity, in the first-class cabins and saloons of the *Conte Grande*, *Conte Rosso*, *Conte Biancamano* and, above all, the *Rex*, showpiece of the Italian merchant marine at the beginning of the thirties. She was to plow the waves, glittering with lights, off the Rimini coast in an evocative scene from Federico Fellini's *Amarcord* of 1974 in which a group of "daredevils" went out on boats at night to wait along her course and were eventually rewarded with the dazzling vision of her passage. On the navy ships *Trento*, *Trieste* and *Duilio*, Poltrona Frau furnishings came to represent the difference in quality between the accommodation

of the officers and that of the rest of the crew, while the VIPs traveling for business or pleasure on the great transoceanic arks saw them as an extension of the privileges that surrounded them wherever they went. This explains the preference accorded to Poltrona Frau by Ducrot over other suppliers who were prepared to go any lengths to get a foot in the door of the lucrative business of fitting out luxury liners. Ducrot made use of Frau leather armchairs and couches in order to exclude any competition in the design and production of these prestigious settings. And this determination on the part of Ducrot turned out to be highly favorable to the fortunes of Poltrona Frau.

"Every city," wrote Crawford Flitch, "has the nature of a prison, but none has so many means of escape as Cagliari. With a subtle air of modesty, it denies its allures and continually invites you to look away from it." Renzo had indeed looked away, taking one of the "many means of escape" from his city, and was just beginning to reap the benefits of his

Images of life on board ship in the thirties: playing golf, masked ball and diving into the swimming pool, from the leaflet of the Lloyd Sabuado shipping company on the ships *Conte Rosso* and *Conte Verde*.
The *Rex* glowing with light off the coast of Rimini in an evocative image from Federico Fellini's wonderful movie *Amarcord*, 1974.

Armchair 143 on board the *Rex* and an advertising postcard from the twenties. On facing page, Frau armchairs in the salons of the transatlantic liners *Rex* and *Conte Rosso* and in the American Bar of the Grand Hotel Excelsior at Varese.

...il nido...

..frau..

judicious efforts when, all of a sudden, in 1926, he died at the age of only forty-six. In his holograph will he left the firm to his twenty-three-year-old son Ugo and his sixteen-year-old daughter Ada Luisa, and in usufruct to his wife Savina Pisati.

The three of them decided to form a *de facto* company and Ugo Frau took over its running. His father Renzo had certainly not skimped on ensuring he received a suitable education and the young man had gone many times to Germany and England to improve his knowledge of their respective languages. Renzo, who in the twenties was regarded in Turin as more than well-off and even owned a Ceirano with a Weina body, had it in mind to make Ugo his successor. Unlike his father, however, Ugo was not by nature suited to assuming any kind of responsibility, and still less that of running a company. He frequented high Turinese society, dressed impeccably and was an accomplished rider. He cultivated the friendship of Gabriele d'Annunzio, whom he took as a model and whose conduct he sought to imitate. D'Annunzio still had ties of affection with Turin, as a consequence of his lapses into movie making and his passion for automobiles. Thus Renzo's son led a glittering and comfortable life, showing no interest whatsoever in the fate of the company that his father had left him. His mother, who unofficially took his place after setting him up with an apartment in the city center and a generous income, assumed personal responsibility for the family concern. Savina Pisati was an energetic woman, with a good head for business. Above all, she had been Renzo's companion and had understood his plans: she put her experience to good use and soon proved up to the task. In 1928, two years after Renzo Frau's death, celebrations were held in Turin to mark the centenary of the birth of Duke Emanuele Filiberto and the tenth anniversary of victory in the Great War. A major exposition was staged at the Valentino. "The park was transformed under the able direction of a group of 'innovative' architects," writes Maria Cristina Tonelli Michail in *Il design in Italia 1925-1943*, "centering on the figures of Giuseppe Pagano, Gino Levi Montalcini and Armando Melis. In 1928 Gino Pestelli wrote about the Turin Exposition, concentrating on its architecturally innovative aspects, and Plinio Marconi in the pages of *Architettura e arti decorative* and an anonymous journalist in those of *La casa bella* did the same. Although consideration

The 904 of 1930, archetype of the modern armchair in a contemporary drawing and on the cover of a Poltrona Frau catalogue.
Felix the Cat and Mickey Mouse sitting in armchairs clearly inspired by the 904.

of this event in terms of its effect on style lies outside the scope of this book, it is worth stressing the 'homogeneity of the architectural inspiration' that underpinned it, with the measured recourse to a language of sober classicism, perhaps influenced by the contemporary work of people like Gunnar Asplund and Heinrich Tessenow and undoubtedly lent substance by the culturally pregnant climate created in Turin by Lionello Venturi, Riccardo Gualino, Felice Casorati… If anything there was too explicit a reference to the demand for moral, and therefore formal rigor sought by Gualino, at the prompting of Venturi, and expressed not only in the works of architecture produced after the war that he championed but also in the skilful juggling of the public and private through which he had shaped Turinese cultural life since the twenties. Thanks to the faith that Gualino himself placed in architecture as a means of formalizing a lifestyle, the figure of the architect gained a new significance as a factor in the definition of art and culture, something that was affirmed by the exposition in Turin."

Between 1924 and 1925 Gualino, proprietor of a chemical industry and well-known patron of the arts, had the furni-

ture for his own house made in the craft workshop of Giacomo Cometti (1863–1938) to a design by Felice Casorati. Between 1927 and 1928 Cometti also made the furniture for the house of the textile manufacturer Bellora at Gallarate. In August 1928 the magazine *Domus* published the silver flatware designed by Carlo Turina (1885–1956), who had been trained by Cometti, and the same year Renzo Frau's friend and collaborator Eugenio Colmo (1885–1967), otherwise known as Golia, was placed in charge of the Fashion and Celebrations section of the exposition. He also designed the "Lady's Day 1928" stand. Felice Casorati (1886–1963), the great artist from Novara who had been living in Turin since

Vanity Fair, replica of the 904 of 1930, in a picture from the catalogue and on the Poltrona Frau stand at the Salone del Mobile in Milan, 1999. On facing page, the Vanity Fair in the Teatro Farnese at Parma, designed by Giovanni Battista Aleotti in 1618.

1918, designed the Textiles Pavilion and Gigi Chessa (1898–1935) those of the Photographers, of the Valli di Lanzo and of the Potters and Glassblowers. From 1928 to 1930, Gino Levi Montalcini (1902–1974) designed and built the Gualino offices on Corso Vittorio opposite the Valentino, while Prampolini, Fillia, Gaudenzi, Gamberti, Ambrosino, Mitsau and Mazzesi designed the pavilion of Futurist Architecture at the exposition.

The year 1928 was a very important one for Poltrona Frau, which on Savina Pisati's initiative was present at the exposition in the "House of Architects," pavilion 36, designed

according to the *Official Catalogue* by Pietro Betta, Maurizio de Rege di Donato, Mario Dezzutti, Gino Levi Montalcini, Arturo Midana, Sandro Molli, Giuseppe Pagano, Mario Passanti, Paolo Perona, Ettore Pittini, Antonio Pogatschnig, Natale Reviglio, Gino Ricci, Giuseppe Rosso and Domenico Soldiero Morelli. Frau furniture was also on show in the pavilion of Futurist Architecture and at the Leather Show in the pavilion of Industry.

According to Daniele Baroni: "At that time the company had for several years been run by Frau's widow. Taking over at a time when the firm's reputation had reached its peak, she was able to keep it at a high level throughout the thirties and until well into the war... The company's advertisements appeared regularly in the two most prestigious Italian architectural magazines of the time, *Domus* and *La casa bella*, the former founded in 1928 and the latter just a few months later… The slogans changed with the times, passing from 'Working is a pleasure when you can sit on a Frau' to 'The prototype of the modern armchair: widely imitated but never equaled' of a decade later. The problem of protecting its brand from the numerous imitations had already presented itself. An advertisement brought out in 1924 contained the following recommendation: 'Beware of imitations, which have nothing in common with the Frau original…' A document dating from 1926, from the office of the duke of Pistoia, a prominent personality in the Turin of the twenties, records Renzo Frau's appointment as supplier to the house, granting him the right to place 'His August Coat of Arms' on his signs. In the meantime Frau had also become regular supplier to the royal palace and to numerous members of the royal family, as well as to politicians and distinguished writers."

One of the most significant testimonials is to be found in a letter written by Sem Benelli, a celebrated playwright of the time, dated December 27, 1923. One of his plays, *La cena delle beffe*, set in Renaissance Florence, was made into a movie in 1941 by the director Alessandro Blasetti. The actors included Amedeo Nazzari in the part of Neri Chiaramantesi and Clara Calamai in that of Ginevra. The beautiful Calamai made an immediate impact, when the irate Neri tore off her blouse and for the first time in the history of the sound film, an actress revealed her bare breasts. Sem Benelli wrote the letter to Renzo from his castle-like villa at Zoagli, which still looms above you as you drive along the Aurelia, standing on a curve and bristling absurdly with battlements. "Dear Signor Frau, only today have I taken your

armchairs out of their crates. Magnificent! As enticing as oblivion! Wonderful colors! Extraordinarily soft in their feminine leather! A man accustomed to all sorts of labors like me can allow himself to be embraced by those voluptuous sirens with a smile! Bravo! Bravo! I remember a Roman count who was not as proud of the classical marbles and Renaissance paintings in his palace as of the modern English armchairs that he possessed. They were certainly no better than the Italian ones you make. I shall sit in them with more pleasure for this reason too. And it will not be laziness, but joyful victory! I shake your hand and congratulate you. Happy New Year!"

In issue no. 2 of *Cultura Moderna, Rivista Mensile Illustrata*, published on February 10, 1929, Guido Marangoni also praised the armchair, placing the emphasis on the most worn-out

Franco Moschini, president of Poltrona Frau, and Giancarla Quacquarini, sales, image and advertising executive. On facing page, detail of the arm and cushion of Vanity Fair.

sort of pleading, and seems to have wanted to pay a posthumous tribute to Renzo Frau, even though he fails to mention his name: "And then came the really excellent idea of cutting off the armchair from the great and confusing flood of tendencies and direct attempts to discover the portentous recipe for twentieth-century furniture, thereby saving it from the unavoidable fate of having to change its appearance every day as happens with all the other furniture in the modern house. Having partly solved the problem of the armchair in this way, the next step was to base its beauty on the solid balance of forms, the simple and naked austerity of line derived directly from the structure without any merely decorative adjuncts, superfluous and illogical when they have no precise static and structural functions... A real achievement in the

stery that enfolds and titillates you with the caress of fine, velvety leather, almost silky in the most select kinds of morocco. The color of this leather covering is the only decorative element that the armchair permits itself to increase its fascination: an endless range of tints and shades and nuances that allows the man of taste to choose the one best-suited to his own home and in harmony with the décor in which the armchairs will be placed." So Savina Pisati had no reason to worry about the company's future when, in 1929, the repercussions of the economic crisis in America, culminating in the Wall Street Crash, were felt in Italy too, as in the whole of Europe. Poltrona Frau did not suffer the reduction in demand that hit its competitors in the early thirties. It had the reputation of an excellent product, both in its construc-

contemporary art of furnishing, perhaps the most useful and important up to now. It has the great merit of fitting in with all the styles, antique and modern, of the other pieces of furniture with which it has to share a setting. And it is aesthetically at home anywhere: in the hall and the drawing room, in the antechamber and the boudoir, on the transatlantic liner and in the grand hotel. On an elegant veranda and in the study of the businessman and the professional... Its sober styling represents the *non plus ultra* of simplification, of logic; and a harmonious synthesis of essential lines. It has the charm of an insuperable intimacy, concerned only with concealing its hard wooden core under a delicately soft uphol-

tion and its materials, and was even considered a collectable, an investment for those who could afford it. It was in just those years that Ducrot subcontracted the supply of furniture for the Italian Parliament to Poltrona Frau. And while Frau did not manage high sales in the north of the peninsula, the results achieved in the south, especially in Campagna and Sicily, were better than the most optimistic forecasts.
In addition, there were good prospects for export to Germany and France, even at a time when, as Guido Piovene (1907–1974) was to comment in the immediate postwar period, between 1947–49, in his dispatches to the *Corriere della Sera* from Paris, that would later be collected in

Tilly Losch and Roman Jasiński at the Savoy Theatre in London in 1933. On facing page, posters from the thirties: by Schawinsky for Olivetti, 1934, Ivrea, private collection; by Dudovich for Borsalino, 1930, Treviso, Museo Civico Luigi Bailo; by Depero for the Società Nazionale Gazometri, 1934, Milan, private collection.

Madame France, "only French furniture is appreciated and has a sure market. Not even English furniture is very popular. And the Venetian style of the eighteenth century is perceived as too bombastic and Oriental. And an Oriental carpet, however beautiful, will always look like a second-class carpet to a Frenchman. With the result that French carpets reach extraordinarily high prices on the domestic market. Even before the war, a large, authentic Savonnerie carpet could fetch several million. Now they are almost unobtainable: the surviving examples are split between the museums and a few stately homes... In this republican country all the fine houses inevitably turn into miniature Versailles: a French drawing room, with hangings on its walls, is a small-scale copy of the French castle surrounded by forest."

In 1934 Savina Pisati bought a plot of land on Via Tripoli in Turin and started work on the construction of a factory. The old stables on Via Modena no longer met the requirements of a rapidly growing company. At the same time she set up a new and larger showroom at no. 12, Via Santa Teresa, giving up the premises on Via Palazzo di Città. But these were changes of a logistic character: her business policy did not diverge from the guidelines established by Renzo, but just amplified and developed them.

Frau furniture was now an unmistakable presence on the domestic scene, a mark of family priorities: armchairs and couches survived, perpetuating the memory of the father, mother, grandfather... "Pieces of furniture, like portraits, are a continuation of our parents, our relatives, our friends, in this world," wrote Alberto Savinio (1891–1952) in *Casa La vita*. "Signor Munster peers though his eyelashes, watching the murky light spread through the room and penetrate between the heavy shadows of the furniture like the sea between a group of rocks." He has just woken up and "resumes his usual morning game, which consists in confusing the shapes of the two armchairs and the couch with the images of his deceased father's family … The two leather armchairs are pop and mom in the last years of their life, the cloth-covered couch is Aunt Zenaide lying prone and draped in her famous housecoat embroidered with floral patterns. Aunt Zenaide's arm is the side cushion of the couch, in the shape of a stubby sausage, the tassel hanging from the sausage her hand, which Munster as a child had had to kiss every night before he went to bed, after kissing Signor Munster his father on his bare and cold skull and Signora Munster his mother on her cheek smelling of henbane, the consequence of a trusty liniment that she used every now

and then to assuage her continuous and excruciating toothaches. Aunt Zenaide's hand, by contrast, smelled of carbolic acid, a sign of her terror of microbes and constant fear of contagion. If she had not been afraid of her brother's mockery, Aunt Zenaide would not have allowed her nephew to touch her hand with 'that mouth which had been in contact with who knows what muck.' That cloth-covered divan prolonged Aunt Zenaide's earthly life and gave shape to her immortality, but it must also be said that even when she was alive and ever since Signor Munster could remember, Aunt Zenaide had always had the personality of a sofa… Signor Munster likes these pieces of furniture for their familiar and human appearance, and he heartily congratulates himself on not having ended up surrounded by 'twentieth-century' furniture that consists of nothing more than chrome-plated skeletons incapable of keeping a man company."

While Frau upholstered furniture had always stood out from whatever style was in fashion, Daniele Baroni points out in reference to Savina Pisati's management of the company that "the new models that were occasionally brought out took on an increasingly 'twentieth-century' and metaphysical tone, with closed and compact forms. Essentially, though, they maintained an unmistakable stylistic continuity." For, as Franco Moschini has observed, "while Savina Pisati displayed undoubted managerial skills, her efforts also showed that Renzo's wife did not confine herself, however prudent her running of the company, to exploiting the legacy of a catalogue of models that had already proved themselves on the market but went far beyond this, seeking to realize the innovative potential of Renzo's ideas about design, which had not found expression as a consequence of his untimely death in 1926. And I believe that he himself already had it in mind to go beyond this first range of successful models, the fruit of formal purification, and was thinking about designing completely new kinds of upholstered furniture, relying on a trademark that would be their best guarantee. And so it was that, in 1930, just four years after his death, Savina Pisati was able to bring into production the 904 which, in its form and substance, confirmed Renzo's intentions. And this is still more comprehensible when, by picking out exemplary models—without any desire to date such timeless objects—we set out to reconstruct the history of production at Poltrona Frau. In 1912 there was the 127, visibly soft as I have already described it in reference to Eugenio Colmo's fanciful and humorous interpretation: in fact Renzo had a poster with the drawing of the Eternal Father posted in all the waiting rooms

The Lira model of 1916 was revised in 1934, when the back was given a rounded shape. The replica of the original 1934 model was given the name Lyra.

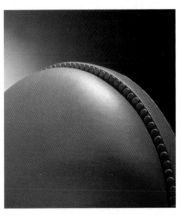

Two ladies at Ascot in 1936 wearing elegant clothing typical of the period.

of the principal Italian railroad stations. The 127 is a comfortable, welcoming form, distinguished by the goose-down cushion that covers the plump half-cylinder back. The 96, on the other hand, from 1915, is more austere, with no cushion, and has a back with a geometric pattern of straps. It is the one that appeared most often in the advertisements carried by *Numero* of Turin. The Lira of 1916 is decidedly of the drawing-room variety, with a velvet cushion. I think that this was at the express desire of the person who first commissioned it, undoubtedly a woman, who refused to place her precious bottom in contact with the hide of an animal. In 1934, nevertheless, Poltrona Frau brought out a version with a rounded back, covered entirely with leather: its current replica is the Lyra. In 1919 there was the 128, with cushion, footrest and book rest. Decidedly a rare example of a prototype and, at the same time, a recapitulation of the upholstered armchair—as it was described on March 4, 1979, by the weekly *L'Espresso*, in reference to our replica: the 1919."

A truly timeless piece of furniture, the 128. We can even imagine it as the armchair in the story *L'incendiario* by Aldo Palazzeschi (1885–1974), who, in *Stampe dell'Ottocento*, conjures up an episode from his life with his mother and leaves out any reference to the date. "One evening in spring, after supper, when I was five years old, the window of the room was open and my mother was sitting in an armchair reading while the maid cleared the table; my father had gone out." The child, the writer, lit some matches and placed them on the window jamb. After scolding the little boy for the indelible marks he had burned into the wood, his mother "had gone back to her armchair and started reading again as if nothing had happened." By settling down comfortably again, the mother minimized what had happened, but the child was left with the fear that his father would discover the marks.

The 128 also appeared in the beautiful poster designed by Nanni, in the mid-twenties, with a woman draped over it languidly, a cigarette in her hand, while the coils of smoke rising from her lips form the word Frau. "The 22," continues Franco Moschini, "does not refer to the year of its birth, 1922. I have personally investigated the meaning of the reference numbers used by Frau, and believe that they must be attributed to the pieces produced, to the date of the inclusion of the individual model in the catalogue. In this case date and year match. The 22 is a comfortable armchair, even though it was designed for a more erect, less slumped posture: decidedly a chair for conversation, not relaxation.

When the 177 of 1925 was placed in the catalogue along with the sofa derived from it, it was the first time that Renzo had presented a coordinated set of furniture. The sofa matched the armchair in the perfect rigor of its form, while the 143 would serve as the basic model for naval supply contracts. The 118 dates from 1929, preceding the 904 by a year in the order of replication: Fumoir, and Vanity Fair, defined as an archetype of the modern armchair. The last two entered into production when Savina Pisati took over the management of the company. And if the form of the first is another example of the purification commenced by Renzo, the second is definitely an expression of the innovative intention that he did not have time to put into effect."

In 1935 Ada Luisa, the daughter of Savina Pisati and Renzo Frau, married Roberto Canziani, a former player for the Inter soccer club and a representative by profession. He was soon given responsibility for sales in the company. In 1938 the shares of Anonima Poltrona Frau, incorporated that year, were split equally between Ada Luisa and Ugo Frau, in fulfillment of Renzo's last wishes. Ugo died in 1940, after a distressing illness, and his shares were acquired by Roberto Canziani: added to those held by his wife, this gave him effective control of the company. The 900A model, Tabarin in the replica, had been in production for four years when Savina Pisati went into retirement and Roberto Canziani, who was already the majority stockholder, personally took over the running of Poltrona Frau.

"The 900A series," comments Franco Moschini, "was the last that can be attributed to Renzo's innovative intentions, taken up and pursued by Savina Pisati. The replica bears the name Tabarin, which refers to the genre of variety song that was contemporary with the years of Poltrona Frau's foundation and development."

A prominent celebrity of the time, "Gino Franzi, around

"The 900A series, of 1939, was the last that can be attributed to Renzo's innovative intentions, taken up and pursued by Savina Pisati." In the background, a detail of Pablo Picasso's *Guernica*, 1937, Madrid, Museo Nacional Centro de Arte Reina Sofia.

TABARIN

design Archivio Frau

Poltrona Frau

Tolentino (Italy)

The replica of the 900A of 1939
is called Tabarin referring
to the variety of song
that was contemporary with the years
of the conception, growth
and developement of Poltrona Frau.

Full view and details of the Tabarin series showing the extreme comfort of the form and the rigor of its profile.

1920," writes Gianni Borgna in *Storia della canzone italiana*, "undisputed master of song, used to appear on stage in a midnight blue tailcoat and stovepipe hat to sing in a baritone voice of his sardonic skepticism about a world that covered up virtue with deception. His *Scettico blues* ('Skeptical Blues') is famous: 'What do I care if the world / has turned me cold? / If in everything at bottom / I find nothing but woe? / Since my first love / shattered my life, / without illusions, I go roaming / round the world… / and laughing at it / mocking my fate…!' The person who most effectively held up the world and songs of the *tabarin* to ridicule was Ettore Petrolini… In *Gastone*, 1921, in which he invented the figure of the 'fop,' which went on to triumph in the humorous magazines of half the world, his irony toward the frivolous and fatuous world of the *tabarin* grew particularly savage: Gastone, a highly photogenic performer in the movies, star turn in variety shows, *danseur*, *diseur* and frequenter of the 'Bal-Tabarin,' inveterate womanizer, man incredibly tired of everything, man of great charm, man ruined by the war. 'Gastone, you are the master of the cinema / Gastone / Gastone./ Gastone, I have women galore / and I collect them / Gastone / Gastone….'"

After giving up control of the company Savina Pisati moved in the early forties to her country house at Castelnuovo Don Bosco. The factory on Via Tripoli and the showroom on Via Santa Teresa were seriously damaged by bombing. Her decision to leave the helm marked the end of Poltrona Frau's golden age in Turin. In fact during the years of postwar reconstruction, and the subsequent economic boom, Roberto Canziani proved unable to cope with the task that he had taken on.

And here it is worth referring once again to the significance of Renzo's legacy: he was a craftsman, and had founded an absolutely craft-based company. He created an image that went well beyond the company's actual production potential, in which the work of the craftsman was mythologized with respect to industrial manufacture. Renzo had placed himself outside the common run, but in exactly the opposite way to Thonet, even though both of them produced models of furniture which would become classics. In his family, only Savina Pisati was capable of being a worthy heir: the 904 is the most significant example of this, and is still a classic today, "molded like a body, stimulating its tactile qualities to a point verging on sensuality." It is not upholstered with leather to cover up imperfections, as its body has a perfect structure. The leather is the last touch necessary to all the components that enrich the wooden frame, in order to attain the definitive form. Thus the 904 is undoubtedly the outcome of a concurrence of passionate voices.

Unfortunately, Roberto Canziani would be unable to exploit the Frau heritage. Right from the start, in fact, he compromised the company's position of undisputed leadership in the sector of upholstered furniture by promoting its image in a confused manner. He took the advertisements out of exclusive architectural magazines and placed them in second-rate publications, as well as stringing up banners with the Poltrona Frau logo in stadiums and at cycle tracks. Canziani disoriented Poltrona Frau's clientele in this way in order to win the attention of different strata of society, and these in turn began to influence the company's output. Their continual demand for modifications only served to damage its credibility. And, while it is true that airplanes had by now replaced transatlantic liners on the route to the New World, closing forever the chapter of refined furnishings for first-class cabins, Poltrona Frau even lost its orders from public institutions, as well as Ciga and the banks, as Canziani, following the disappearance of the intermediary Ducrot, was unable to establish new relationships that would have allowed the company to carry on in this area.

Thus as the income from the few local contracts—furnishings for the RAI offices, the private rooms in the Delle Molinette hospital and some branches of the Banco di Sicilia in Turin—dried up, the Frau coffers inevitably began to empty. In 1958, the company's heavy indebtedness to the banks forced Canziani to sell the whole of the property on Via Tripoli, which included not only the factory and offices but also a spacious and luxurious apartment that Savina Pisati had had built for the family. He transferred production and the administration offices to rented premises at no. 10, Via Bizozzero. In 1959 his son Ugo was killed in a road accident at the age of just eighteen. Canziani was devastated by the tragedy and the company was left to its own devices until 1962, the year when he seems to have seriously intended to file for bankruptcy.

Among its creditors, the most exposed was the Conceria del Chienti at Tolentino, in the province of Macerata in the Marche, a tannery that belonged to a group of companies run by the Nazareno Gabrielli family. The tannery had been supplying hides to Poltrona Frau since before the Second World War and, though aware of the difficulties faced by the Canziani management, did not cut off supplies, trusting in the brand's reputation. Faced with a choice between losing the whole of the tannery's credit or acquiring Poltrona Frau in its parlous state, the Gabrielli decided on the latter option and gave Franco Moschini, who had just married into the family, the job of carrying out the takeover.

"I realized at once that my task went well beyond supervising the takeover, which was going to be a long and bureaucratic process, and in any case a delicate and difficult one, even dramatic at certain moments," recalls Franco Moschini. "Canziani's place had been taken by his daughter Donatella, and she had tried in vain to put the company back on its feet, after it had reached the end of the line in the cramped premises at no. 7 Via Pascoli in Turin. But I saw that the trademark 'Poltrona Frau' had really been branded into the memory of all those who had dealt in or bought Renzo's armchairs. So I had to understand the reasons for this in order to be able to find the best and most consistent way to revive the company. Curiously, rather than hurting the name, the debacle had given it an even greater resonance, and so it was my job to bring it back under effective management that would be able to exploit this fact. I immediately thought that the way to do this was to track down the models that had helped to create the Frau legend, to try to understand their formal significance and criteria of construction and if possible to reproduce them, making the necessary retouches in order to bring them up to date. And it was at this point that my admiration for Renzo's accomplishment began to grow, a feeling that remains unchanged today."

Thus in 1962 Franco Moschini set out to pick up the thread of a continuity of design, searching with great difficulty for its end amidst the rubble of the company that had collapsed fifty years after its foundation. Once he had got a firm grasp on it, he began laying the foundations for the rebirth of Poltrona Frau.

Curiously, this was the very year in which the Turin-based Einaudi Editore published *Il giardino dei Finzi Contini* (*The Garden of the Finzi-Continis*) by Giorgio Bassani (1916–2000). The book covers the period from the middle of the thirties until the early forties and in his description of Professor Ermanno's house, the author distinguishes the furniture that had accumulated there over the course of time from the ones in the studio of Micol's brother Alberto: "Monumental cabinets, heavy seventeenth-century settles with lion's feet, tables of the kind you find in a refectory, leather-covered Savonarola chairs with bronze studs, Frau armchairs, complicated glass or iron light fixtures hanging from coffered ceilings, thick carpets in shades of tobacco, carrot and ox-blood covering darkly gleaming parquets. There was, perhaps, a larger quantity of nineteenth-century pictures, landscapes and portraits, and of books, many of them bound, in rows behind the glass panes of large bookcases of dark mahogany... With him leading the way and me trailing behind, we walked through at least a dozen rooms of different sizes, some of them as big as true halls, others small, even tiny, and linked together by corridors that were not always straight or on the same level. Finally, in the middle of one of these corridors, Professor Ermanno stopped in front of a door. 'Here we are,' he said. He gestured at the door with his thumb and winked... I entered. 'Ah, you're here?' Alberto greeted me. He was slumped in an armchair. He raised himself by pushing down on the arms with both hands, got to his feet, placed the book he was reading with its spine upward on a low table alongside and at last came to meet me...'You like the way I've set up the studio?' asked Alberto. He suddenly seemed anxious to win my approval, which I did not begrudge him of course. I lavished praise on the simplicity of the furniture (getting up, I had gone to take a closer look at a large drawing table set crosswise near the window and surmounted by a perfect metal lamp with an articulated arm), and in particular on the indirect lighting which I 'said' I found not only restful but also ideal for working. He let me talk and appeared content. 'Did you design the furniture?' 'Well, no. I copied them partly from *Domus* and *Casabella* and partly from *Studio*, you know, the English magazine... They were made for me by a little joinery shop on Via Coperta.' Hearing me express my approval of his furniture—he added—could not but fill him with satisfaction. Whether I wanted to relax or work, in fact, what need was there to surround myself with ugly things or old junk?"

Franco Moschini was convinced, from the start, of the need to keep Poltrona Frau away from the jumble of pseudo-antique furniture that glutted the market at that time. The Frau classics had nothing to do with that hodgepodge of inevitably dated models. Yet he had to go further than his initial task and could not come up with something new by copying it from architectural magazines like the "little joinery shop on Via Coperta" in Ferrara in Bassani's novel. He had to establish a dialogue with the most astute designers, on the basis of a project of continuity, whose thread he had so laboriously picked up again.

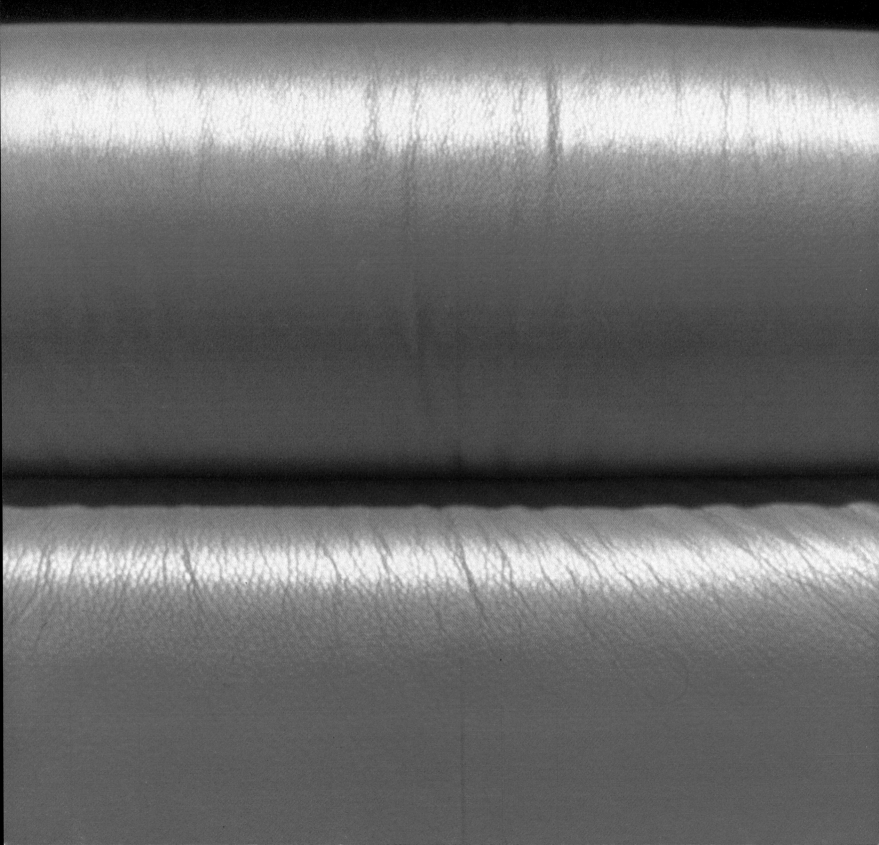

Models and Modes of Frau Living
From Dezza to I Madrigali

"My hair was never covered with sawdust, and neither had I breathed the pungent smell of glue. At that time, in the temple of the trade, charming Brianza, the only guarantee of a furniture maker's reliability was if he had waste material all over him. So I was clearly not born to the craft," recalls Franco Moschini, "at least the way they saw it in Meda. My background was in the building trade, where my responsibilities were of an administrative nature and, I must confess, I had come to the conclusion that I was better suited to building houses than to undermining their foundations. In Macerata they say: in life there are 'those who pile up and those who knock down.' I identify with the former, which makes material sense, clearly discernible in those age-old dry-stone walls that are used to mark the boundaries of properties in the countryside in those parts. It was with this spirit that I agreed to take on Frau and, as a first move, I had decided to leave the company's registered office in Turin but move the production, administrative and commercial facilities to Tolentino. Of the five workers who were still on the pay bill at Via Pascoli, just one chose to come with me, the only one who wasn't put off by the idea of going to the Marche, so remote from his world and his habits. He was the one who was going to train a workforce in the new location and who would be promoted to foreman, in the field. There was no tradition of upholstered furniture in Tolentino, but there was one of tanning, even if there is a profound difference between the types of leather used to make wallets, shoes and bags and the ones used to cover armchairs. It was a moment of transition, and a difficult one: in Turin the few remaining orders were filled, while

the conditions were created in Tolentino for the development of the new production facility. Since 1928, in fact, the Gabrielli family had been living in a house whose bottom two floors were occupied by the factory of the same name. We took advantage of the opportunity provided by the transfer of the latter to new premises to set up Poltrona Frau in the rooms that were left empty. Then I managed, through a common acquaintance, to get in touch with Gio Ponti. I was aware of the quality of his work and commissioned him to design a range that I hoped to be able to use for hotel contracts, which had accounted for a substantial part of the company's turnover in Renzo's time and under Pisati's management."

Moschini felt that Poltrona Frau had to make it clear right from the start that it intended to maintain continuity with the line of formal research that had commenced in the thirties with the 904 and, as Vittorio Gregotti pointed out in *Il disegno del prodotto industriale: Italia 1860-1980*, "Gio Ponti, with his great activism (but also with his remarkable flair for design had led him as early as 1948 to devote his attention to the Pavone coffeemaker and the Visetta sewing machine), remained the fundamental go-between… Linked in his

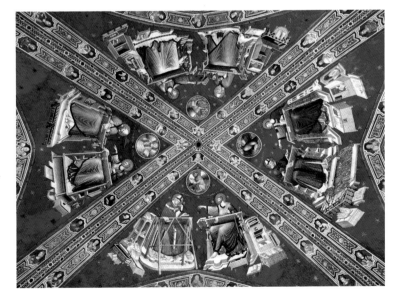

Detail of the ceiling of the Cappellone di San Nicola di Tolentino (Macerata).

Two images symbolic of the sixties: the Beatles, in a photograph taken in 1964, and Andy Warhol's painting *Colored Campbell's Soup Can*, 1965, private collection.
On facing page, Dezza designed by Gio Ponti in 1965; the gold plaque of the International Competition for Hotel Furniture, Tecnhotel, 1966, awarded to Gio Ponti's Dezza range.

approach to design to the styles of Campigli and Fiumi, Ponti was in figurative and sociological terms the ideal intermediary with prewar bourgeois culture... It was only in those years that he began to make unexpected ventures into the modern figurative world or, rather, into modern 'style.' There can be no doubt that his most significant contribution remains the 'Superleggera' chair, inspired by the traditional work of the Chiavari and designed for Cassina in a series of versions up until the definitive one of 1957."

In 1965 Gio Ponti (1887–1979) designed the Dezza series for Poltrona Frau. This is how he explained the reasoning behind it: "What should a modern armchair be like? What are its fundamental requisites? First of all it ought to be comfortable, like armchairs in the good old days, and therefore the expression of a precise function, but at the same time an expression of the ideas of a designer, and for this reason modern. In a personal accent that derives from the concepts that have given rise to its elements. So it should be very strong but light, easy to move around and fit into any setting, be it a private home, study, public place, hotel, as long, of course, as the décor is an expression of modern taste. It should be presented in a select range of colors and perfectly constructed. From the technical viewpoint, it should be easy to produce and to ship, made so that it can be dismantled in order to go anywhere. Finally, it should be put on the market at a competitive price."

The Dezza series was presented at the third Tecnhotel hotel show at Genoa in 1966 and was awarded the gold plaque, first prize in the International Competition for Hotel Furniture. This was at a time when, as Gio Ponti himself commented with reference to the Eurodomus exhibition in issue no. 440 of *Domus*, brought out that same year: "Trade Fairs reflect the market as it really is. They are the market free to express itself. They are like a page of a newspaper on which you find everything that is part of daily life—i.e. perennial: acts of generosity, and criminality, heroism and cowardice, the beautiful and the ugly, the sublime and the horrible, genius and stupidity, order and disorder, lucidity and obtuseness. But the Trade Fairs also have sections in which you can find everything, yet all of it is based on intel-

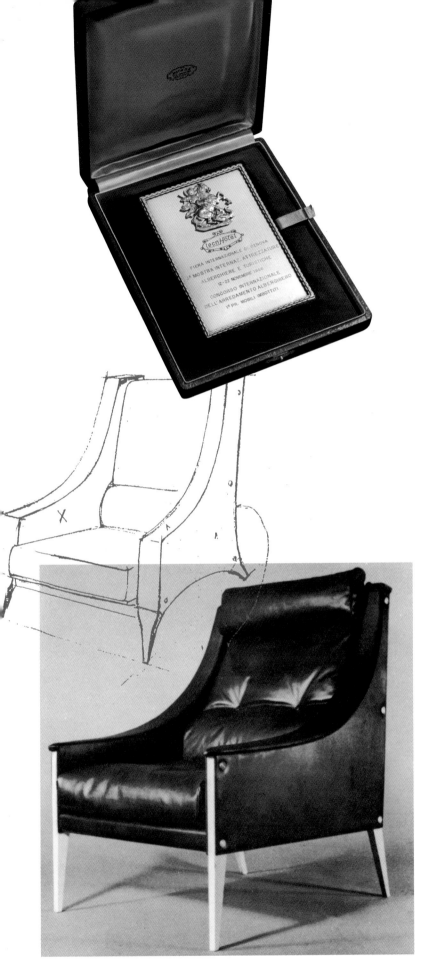

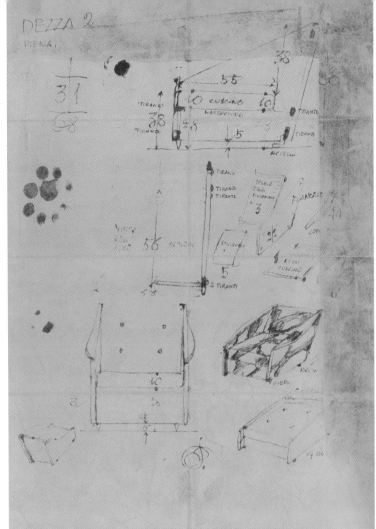

The modern armchair "should be very strong but light... fit into any setting, be it a private home..., public place, hotel," stated Gio Ponti about the Dezza series.
Frank Stella, *Ossippee I*, 1966.
New York, private collection.

ligent research. Everything works, everything is for the best, everything is in regular production, everything is at a competitive price, everything answers to a need, everything is progressive. These are the sections of machinery: you won't find a stupid machine, a machine that doesn't work, a machine that is not in perfect and constant production, a machine that is no use. And the public that visits these sections, though fairly small in number (like the one that visits the agricultural sections), is an intelligent public, capable of judging whether the machine meets their needs, whether it is worth its price. Here there are no preconceptions. In the field of furniture it is different. For here the public has preconceptions, and *vult decipi* wants to be deceived, i.e. wants the fake, the mediocre, the copy, the object that looks luxurious but isn't, and it places more value on what it believes something to be than what it actually is. While there is no need to educate the buyer of machinery, this is not true where furniture is concerned. In any case, what Eurodomus set out to do was to present effective solutions, at competitive prices, designed by designers and answering practical needs; and in this it was necessary to identify a style. This is the road to take, and the first step on it shows that it is worth proceeding."

Gio Ponti had founded *Domus* in 1928 and had been its editor up until 1940, only to take over the helm again from 1948 to 1978. His diagnosis looks even more accurate and specific when seen in relation to the experience with Poltrona Frau. Dezza could undoubtedly be said to correspond completely to its designer's declaration of intent but, to use his own words, the public "places more value on what it believes something to be than what it actually is." And yet the series formed a fine range of armchairs and couches that could easily have been used for public places, or as individual pieces in the home. Testimony to this is provided by the various components of which it was made up: Dezza 12, Dezza 24, Dezza 36 and their relative couches, Dezza 48. While the

first, low and trim, allowed two or more armchairs to be put together, owing to the particular conformation of the arms, the next two were intended to be placed alongside the couches, differing from one another in the positioning of their arms. The 48 on the other hand, was a high armchair, with a headrest fitted to its back. However it was hard for the public, most of whom were still buying period furniture, to comprehend Dezza, and Poltrona Frau did not yet have the kind of sales outlets that were required to attract more sophisticated customers.

On the other hand, even Karl Mang, in his *The History of Modern Furniture*, took care to clarify the attitude of that section of the public which, from the middle of the nineteenth century up until our own day, has accounted for the most substantial part of the market for furniture. "Ever since the baroque era, it has been the custom of the upper classes of society to entrust architects not just with the construction of their homes, but also with their furnishing, or to order it from craftsmen who were able to provide furniture suited to the style of the building. Since the middle of the nineteenth century, the time when the architecture of rented apartments took off, broader strata of the population have sought social recognition through imitation of the nobility and upper middle class. The manufacturers of furniture, organized on the principles of the division of labor even if not yet completely industrialized, soon brought out a vast range of furniture designed and produced in a uniform style, for the furnishing of particular settings. Their dimensions were suited to the proportions of the recently constructed rented apartments. Reproductions of antique furniture, followed by Jugendstil designs adapted for production in small runs, appeared more and more frequently, in step with the growing pace of industrialization, in manufacturers' catalogues. This type of furniture has

Luigi Massoni's Lullaby bed of 1968, with the Criss Cross container and the chair of the Dilly Dally dressing table. On facing page, a fashion show with Lurex dresses in the sixties.

retained its function of 'embellishment' to the present day. With their simulation of a higher social status these pieces of furniture, too large and heavy for today's apartments, have taken away precious living space and continue to dominate a large part of the market." And don't be deceived into thinking that the reference to "Jugendstil" means that this diagnosis only applied to the furniture market in Germany. Even today, the situation remains much the same in a large part of Europe.

"In the light of how the market was going to develop," comments Franco Moschini, "Dezza truly anticipated the more optimistic predictions about the evolution of demand. We were made aware of this even by the upheaval that it caused in the factory. Dezza was not just an armchair, it was an authentic system of construction based on finished components, to be assembled afterward in accordance with demand. It therefore entailed the maintenance of a stock, and of individual semifinished and finished products, and a genuine assembly line. The system had nothing to do with the Frau tradition of the armchair seen as a monolith. I had to separate Dezza, as it distanced itself from the classic collection, and entitle the series 'Frau New Line.' But I realized that only a very small part of the orders from hotels and public bodies could be filled with the new series, while demand was growing for the models that stood for Poltrona Frau's more familiar identity. So I had to start off, just as Renzo had done in his own time, by making suitable retouches, updating those models and putting them onto the market as completely up-to-date pieces. It was my meet-

ing with Luigi Massoni that got the operation under way." Thus it was a question of a simple, minimal updating of the form, without any substantial modification of the traditional criteria of furniture construction that were now taking root among Poltrona Frau's workers at Tolentino. And it was precisely that culture that Franco Moschini proposed to make the most of when he met Massoni in 1966. The architect agreed with him and accepted the undertaking. It was certainly not easy to do this in a context where the tradition of upholstered furniture was wholly absent. One is reminded of the difficulties encountered by the hero of Carlo Sgorlon's novel *La poltrona*, published in those years, a teacher who was convinced that he could improve the quality of his life by making himself a present of an armchair that would at last be really comfortable, which he set out to build with his own hands. Fortunately, teachers of literature only try their hands at upholstery in the imagination of the Friulian writer. "It will be hard to pull

it off, but I must. The pieces are there, I've already spent the money on the wood and having it sawn, and I don't throw money away. That armchair has to be built. I've spent winter after winter always in bed, in this bloody house. Half of my notes have been written in bed: that bed weighs on me like a nightmare. Enough. Whatever it costs me I have to finish the armchair. I don't care a jot about the homework. I've got time after the vacation anyway, as I don't have to give them their marks until January 11. Now the armchair. I know what I'm like, I won't get any peace until I've done it. I start to tremble inside, with fever. Something gets going inside me that I just can't stop. Enough of the bed, it's all over with the bed." The obsession with the armchair becomes almost physical and takes up the whole of the teacher's day during his Christmas vacation.

"It's difficult to know where's the best place to start. You'd need to be a joiner, to have a bit of experience, to have seen how joiners do it at least once. I'll start with a leg, not a very risky piece. I put it in the vice but the wood is very soft and the vice cuts into it. I mustn't make it too tight. Now it'll take elbow grease with the rasp. First the rough rasp, then the fine one, then the file and lastly the sandpaper. Almost at once I start sweating, and I soon realize that it's going to take longer than I thought. Forty minutes and more have already gone by on one leg, and that's just to rasp it. Now I have to start with the sandpaper. No, it's better to shape everything with the rasp first and then sand them all together: the production line is more efficient. It's true that it is less satisfying: finishing one thing at a time is very different, you get a sense of the

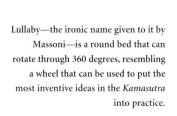

Lullaby—the ironic name given to it by Massoni—is a round bed that can rotate through 360 degrees, resembling a wheel that can be used to put the most inventive ideas in the *Kamasutra* into practice.

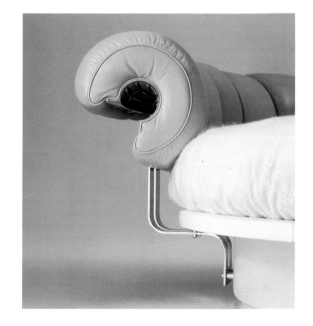

object taking shape, you see it growing under your eyes. I like that too, I have the craftsman's spirit. Who knows how many generations of craftsmen I'm descended from? The legs have turned out quite well, they have a fine shape. I work on them with the sandpaper, but I'm already drenched with sweat... Forget about the legs, I'm fed up with them and my arms ache too much. Now I'll start on the frame for the seat. Let's hope it goes well, because the joints are no joke. Quite the opposite: they're the most difficult thing of all, because they have to be absolutely precise. What's needed is a machine, who knows if I'll manage? Now I have to finish the armchair, it's got to be ready tomorrow... I've almost finished the first joint, now I'll try it out. Of course it doesn't work, the tongue won't fit into the groove. I've been too careful. Afraid it would be loose, I've made it too big and now I'm going to have to rasp it. No, not with the rasp, with the rasp it'll come out curved. I should pare it down with the chisel instead. I give it two blows with the chisel and try it. It's big, it's still too big. I cut another slice and at last it looks right. It fits perfectly, indeed it's still just a bit big because I have to hit it with the hammer to make it go in. Let's hope I don't break the groove, that's all I'd need... I've made the second joint. This

A dynamic image of the Dilly Dally mini dressing table.

time the tongue should be right, I haven't made it so large this time. I try it. It's loose. I should have known, it was bound to happen. First I make it too big and then too small. I'll have to glue on a strip of wood. I look for the adhesive and can't find it."

The teacher looks everywhere and in the end finds the adhesive. And, after making the remaining joints, starts on the gluing: "I spread adhesive on all the joints, tongue and groove, and drive them in with the hammer. Two go in at once and the other two don't want to. This is crazy, first they were fine and now they don't fit. Maybe I waited too long and the adhesive has made them swell up. Perhaps I should have glued them one at a time. I'm going to have to take two of them apart and do it quickly too, before the glue sets, otherwise not even the hammer will get them out. I clean off the adhesive with a rag, give it a once over with the sandpaper and try again. They're still a bit tight, and a bit of glue is left. Another bit of sanding and now they're fine. Wait a

the senses and of that set of aesthetic feelings that characterize the desire of human beings to construct a setting for themselves which, while it may artificial, is still in tune with their bodies. This, in brief, is the poetic and working credo of Luigi Massoni." This is how Anty Pansera described the architect in *Pioniere della via marchigiana al design*. And in reference to his long collaboration with the Gruppo Guzzini of Recanati, which began in 1962 and continues to this day: "'The Le Grazie establishment,' recalls Massoni in a videotaped interview, 'was small, but the people had big ideas: they didn't want to stay where they were, they wanted to do something. Talking about design in those years was just a utopia: the English term seemed to cover up something that nobody understood, something unfamiliar but extraordinary. The profession of designer did not exist, it was just a dream imported from Germany, from America. Designers were people of goodwill for whom architecture was not enough,

minute, I've put one piece in the wrong way round, idiot that I am. I didn't even mark them, I should have put a pencil mark on the right side. By doing things in a hurry I always end up losing more time. I must take every possible precaution so that I don't make a mistake. What should I do? I don't remember, my head feels heavy, my back hurts. It's all this hard work. I don't remember because I'm too tired."
Unlike Gio Ponti who, with Dezza, aimed to supersede the traditional manual approach, Luigi Massoni set out to make the most of its potential by designing forms best suited to bringing out its timeless quality. "Thinking with all ten fingers: which means designing in a way that takes account of

they wanted to broaden the field of their activity.'" But if design was a dream imported "from Germany, from America," what sort of poetics had that dream given rise to in Europe and on the other side of the Atlantic hitherto?
"While in Scandinavia the development of new technical forms," writes Karl Mang, "was only partly interrupted by the Second World War, the major movement that had emerged in Germany lost its most significant exponents after Hitler's rise to power. After the forced closure of the Bauhaus at Dessau in 1932 and its brief interlude in Berlin, Walter Gropius, Marcel Breuer, Ludwig Mies van der Rohe and others emigrated to the United States... With the end of the

Lullaby, Dilly Dally and Criss Cross, as
individual objects, complete in themselves,
do not constitute accessories in a consistent
style: they are pieces of furniture in their
own right, like the armchairs and couches.

Second World War, in Western Europe, the nationalistic
influence of the dictatorships was gone, but in the majority
of countries the destruction caused by the war meant that
they had to start again from scratch... The European furniture industry, to the extent that it had escaped being wiped
out, through submission to the constraints of fascist ideolo-
gy and the priorities of wartime production, had been
unable to develop new ideas or take on new materials. It was
faced instead with North American industry, intact and
dynamic, which was rapidly assuming, largely under the
guidance of important European designers and architects, a
leading role in the furniture sector as well… In any case the
most direct impetus came from the competition 'Organic
Design in Home Furnishings,' held back in 1941 by the
Museum of Modern Art on the initiative of the
Bloomingdale Department Store in New York. The first
prizes for seating went to the team headed by Charles Eames
(born in 1907) and to Eero Saarinen (1910–61). The models
of chair proposed by these two architects—three-dimensional calyxes—led, through the elimination of the right angle,
from the formal world of the two-dimensional curved chairs
of Breuer and Aalto into the new realm of 'sculptural furniture,' whose technology was founded on very recent
advances. Up until the sixties the greater part of the furniture

Late sixties: the moon landing reported on the front page of the *New York Times*, July 21, 1969. Pacifist movements in America and flower children.

produced by Herman Miller's company, in collaboration with Charles Eames, could be traced back to the results of that competition. Without the efforts of that company, which was still of a decidedly limited importance at the time, the evolution that within a short space of time made the United States the leading country in the sector of modern furniture would not even have been possible. In an essay published in a catalogue, George Nelson, who had also worked in close collaboration with Herman Miller, described the latter's company in the following terms: 'It is a small company, in a small city, and is run by its owners. It is distinguished from other ventures in the field by the following principles: 1) what you do is important; 2) design is an essential component of our activity; 3) the product has to be honest; 4) you are the one who decides what you want to produce; 5) there is a market for good design. The plan is to create a permanent collection. This means that each piece is produced until it is no longer in step with the times or can be improved…' For the first time since the Thonet chair, the industry had the possibility of choosing models from a large quantity of experimental chairs and putting them into mass production. Although only some of Charles Eames's prototypes were mass produced by Miller, all these models played a role of decisive importance in the design of furniture over the next twenty years… As early as 1943 Eero Saarinen had started to work for Hans (1914–1955) and Florence Knoll (born in 1917), who had been designers themselves. In 1951 Knoll Associates set up branches in Germany and France, and in 1955 started to produce the furniture that Mies van der Rohe had designed before the war. Over the following years the company collaborated with a series of distinguished designers: Harry Bertoia and, after its takeover of the Italian firm Gavina, Vico Magistretti, Tobia Scarpa and others. Even the furniture designed by Marcel Breuer in the twenties and thirties which had been manufactured by Gavina was brought into mass production by Knoll."

Karl Mang then goes on to describe the scene in Europe: "In Germany, however, a great deal of time was needed, after the total defeat and the destruction of all the major cities, before it was possible to think about more than the satisfaction of primary needs and return to thinking about a modern way of living. Despite all the—politically influenced—attempts to revive the theories of the thirties and their promotion of a functional and inexpensive kind of furniture, like the programs of the WK (Wohnkultur, "culture of habitation") in Germany or the SW (Soziales Wohnen, "social habitation")

Early seventies: a detail of Peter Max's anti-smoking poster for the American Cancer Society of New York and the Smoking armchair, 1970, designed by Sergio Mazza and Giuliana Gramigna. On facing page, student protest in Milan in 1974.

in Austria, the furnishings and décor of the now prosperous middle class and the working class, which was profiting from the favorable economic situation, were characterized by a new eclecticism. Part of the reason for this was that large sections of the population, in a world grown much smaller, were exposed to the furnishings of foreign countries and imitated them blindly. The result was a kitsch that, without any feeling for the new needs that stemmed from the changing historical conditions, was propagated through the illustrated magazines and television… In Denmark things went differently: Arne Jacobsen's reflections on 'doing it a little better,' made the furniture of the International Style accessible to a broader public and offered a significant alternative to the 'teak style.' The work of Poul Kjaerholm (born in 1929) and Jørn Utzon (born in 1918) has to be assessed in the same way. In Germany the design of the International Style was given a theoretical underpinning at the Hochschule für Gestaltung in Ulm, largely through the efforts of Hans Gugelot (1920–1965). The emphasis was placed on aesthetic questions and contemporary social problems… In Italy, a country where the designer had until recently received no scientific training, a number of experiments of great signifi-

"Smoking was our response to the intention of maintaining the characteristics of the leather armchair: soft and comfortable."

"The idea of turning the curve of t
arm inward and of extending the sides
all the way down to the ground allowed
us to define the form."

cance proved particularly successful: the type-writers designed for Olivetti by Marcello Nizzoli and the conception and production of the Vespa and Lambretta in 1948 and 1949. These examples of excellent design also had an influence on the manufacture of furnishings for the home. In the fifties—the period in which the Triennial Exhibitions in Milan, hitherto dominated by artists, increasingly turned their attention to design, and the Milanese group of La Rinascente department stores, with the award of the first Compasso d'Oro prize, began to play a prominent role in the evolution of modern and functional furniture—the foundations were laid for a development of great breadth. Of the numerous and significant designs, which often aroused international interest through publication in the specialist press, only a few were actually brought into production. In spite of the fact that designer objects, demanding and expensive since they were produced in small runs, were only accessible to a few, the creative ideas were so per-

suasive that very soon everyone was talking about the success of Italian products. The designers generally started out from aesthetic solutions, from a plastic conception that was in stark contrast to the rigorous constructivism of the International Style. Their mass-produced articles were designed with an extreme attention to form, verging on the mannered at times, but always convincing in their formulation and marked by a high degree of individualism… Italian furniture owes its existence to an extraordinarily intense collaboration between entrepreneurs, small craft workshops and progressive designers."

Franco Moschini and Luigi Massoni certainly represented one of the most significant examples of the extraordinarily intense collaboration referred to by Karl Mang. "In those days I was rereading," recalls Luigi Massoni, "one of the books I had loved in my youth, a great, timeless book."

Ivan Goncharov (1812–1891) portrays his hero Ilya Ilyitch Ilich Oblomov as devoid of any enterprise: "He was a fellow of a little over thirty, of medium height, and of pleasant exterior. Unfortunately, in his dark-gray eyes there was an absence of any definite idea, and in his other features a total lack of concentration. Suddenly a thought would wander across his face

with the freedom of a bird, flutter for a moment in his eyes, settle on his half-opened lips, and remain momentarily lurking in the lines of his forehead. Then it would disappear, and once more his face would glow with a radiant insouciance which extended even to his attitude and the folds of his night-robe. [...] Even when excited, his actions were governed by an unvarying gentleness, added to a lassitude that was not devoid of a certain peculiar grace.

On the other hand, should depression of spirits show itself in his face, his glance would grow dull, and his brow furrowed, as doubt, despondency, and apprehension fell to contending with one another. Yet this crisis of emotion seldom crystallized into the form of a definite idea—still less into that of a fixed resolve. Almost always such emotion evaporated in a sigh, and shaded off into a sort of apathetic lethargy. [...] With Oblomov, lying in bed was neither a necessity (as in the case of an invalid or of a man who stands badly in need of sleep) nor an accident (as in the case of a man who is feeling worn out) nor a gratification (as in the case of a man who is purely lazy). Rather, it represented his normal condition."

So one cold day he was lying on his bed, in his dressing gown, his room in complete disorder. And "how long he would have remained in this state of indecision it is impossible to say had not a ring at the doorbell resounded through the hall [...]. He gazed curiously toward the door. [...] There entered a young fellow of about twenty-five. Beaming with health and irreproachably dressed to a degree which dazzled the eye [...]. 'Good morning, Volkov!' cried Oblomov. 'And good morning to you,' returned the radiant gentleman, approaching the bed [...]. Volkov hummed the concluding words, and seated himself carelessly upon a chair. Almost instantly he leaped to his feet again, and brushed the dust from his trousers. 'What quantities of dirt you keep everywhere!' he remarked."

Massoni explains the relevance of Ivan Goncharov in the following terms: "I realized that his novel was timeless when I saw how the simple gesture of brushing off the dust was used to distinguish the young man's behavior from that of the hero, even more effectively than the wonderful portrait of him the writer had painted earlier on. I took that gesture as my starting point: I had to free Frau furniture from the layer of dust that made it no longer up to date and restore beauty and youth to those armchairs, to those couches drowsing in the attic. Not, of course, to help out the incorrigible Oblomovs or the characters who, in Sgorlon's book, spend their days trying to deal with their alienation. I had to make those armchairs attractive to the younger generation who had never sat on a Frau."

And perhaps Luigi Massoni was thinking of those lines by Giuseppe Ungaretti (1888-1970) in *C'era una volta*— "Cappuccio Wood / has a slope / of green velvet / like a soft / armchair"—when, introduced to Moschini by Adolfo Guzzini, he commenced his collaboration with Poltrona Frau, in 1966. "I wanted to bring back armchairs and couches that were sensual in their warm colors, in the soft feel of the leather." This was a bold and shrewd

The Poppy armchair, 1975, designed by Tito Agnoli. The same year the ballet *Le Corsaire* was performed in New York.

choice, identifying Frau with the novelty of the product "presented and advertised—and this too was Massoni's idea—in catalogues with well-designed graphics (by Ennio Lucini and Mimmo Castellano)," notes Anty Pansera, "and with an extraordinarily fine set of illustrations."

Massoni himself recalls: "In order to bring the pieces in the historic collection up to date, the first thing I thought of was to revise those details—height, legs, and so on—that no longer seemed suited to the time. And these small changes were enough to reveal the authenticity of those timeless chairs. Then I had a series of colors prepared that were a distinct innovation with regard to the normal livery of Frau armchairs: black and buff. White, fuchsia, yellow, light blue and green conveyed a sense of warmth. At this point, I asked Franco to revive the whole of Renzo Frau's approach to advertising, from the commercial art to the advertisements in magazines to the postcards, even the trademark. And with the help of Ennio Lucini and Mimmo Castellano I set out to create the right image. For I was convinced that it too, and not just the models in production, should communicate a sense of that continuity of design that still distinguishes Poltrona Frau today. Then, one fine day, Franco and I looked at each other: and now? We have to go further, you have to start designing, Franco told me. And what? We agreed on the need to make a choice. The majority of dealers were still selling furniture that was a variation on every possible style of the past, and they put them in their warehouses, not on show, just piled one on top of the other. Out of their total ignorance they had seen the Frau armchairs and couches in the same way

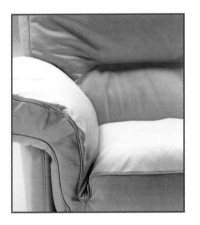

and they refused to accept the collection, now that it was inevitably dissociating itself from the furniture that made up their range of proposals. In those years, however, a new category was emerging and becoming established, that of the quality sales outlet. By this term was meant the showrooms, and not the warehouses, of those dealers who had chosen to sell international designer furniture. They had names like Stilearredo, Ambienti, Spazio Casa, etc. It was to them that we had to turn, and give them a clear signal: we declared that the Frau conception of upholstered furniture was in no way an impediment to design. On the contrary, it would favor its development, not being linked to any period. Proof of this lay in the collection of replicas: the classics. The next step was 'Lullaby,' which won itself a place in the shop windows of the best sales outlets in 1968. With the replicas we had offered confirmation of the Frau conception of armchairs and couches. Now we were affirming the concept of design with new pieces that were intended for use in various parts of the house, so as not to confine the culture of Frau furnishing to the living room. Yet if that famous public full of prejudices, as Gio Ponti had described it, was now beginning to accept design, even if only to a very limited extent, it was still addicted to the most conventional forms of eclecticism in the bedroom. So we decided to tackle this head on by proposing a round bed, set in the middle of the room,

rotating so that it could be oriented to suit the light. And the small 'Criss Cross' containers, on castors. And 'Dilly Dally,' the mini-dressing table with its own small chair. It was an unequivocal signal: good old upholstered furniture could even be used in totally new situations. While the individual pieces were still the fruit of skilled craftsmanship and quality leather and materials. In 1969 I opened a showroom on Via Durini in Milan, which I called 'Centro Forme.' And all the companies from the Marche with which I had collaborated were represented: Poltrona Frau, Design House Guzzini, Nazareno Gabrielli, Fratelli Guzzini and Soprani. In that center, in the heart of the city that was the stronghold of international design, it was possible to attract the interest of the best exporters of products 'made in Italy.' So very soon Poltrona Frau, along with the other brands, became familiar abroad. Then I started to bring in new designers, turning to those I most admired, to flesh out the catalogue, and in the meantime I added other pieces of my own design."

Franco Moschini recalls the collaboration with Luigi Massoni with great affection. "I knew I needed the right partner. Adolfo Guzzini introduced me to Luigi, who was already collaborating with the family in Recanati: we hit it off right away. His idea of emphasizing the noble qualities of leather as a material by adopting a new range of colors not only confirmed its excellence, but brought in a whole new

kind of fascination. It threw an unfamiliar and suggestive light on couches and armchairs, accentuating the potential impact of their softness and comfort. Curiously, the color range invented by Massoni included black and buff, the so-called natural tints. If leather was to be a symbol of the company's production, as it had been for Renzo, then it was my job to ensure that Poltrona Frau had the best quality.

And here I could really score points, even over Renzo, as in his day the tanning of hides was not so sophisticated in all its phases, especially when it came to dyeing, where the color was not yet fully incorporated. We realized this when we looked at the original models, the samples that had been recovered during our reconstruction of the firm's past production. Now there are as many as twenty phases in the dressing process. *Soaking*, which allows the leather, in our case exclusively cowhide, to recover some of the water lost in the salting phase. *Liming* eliminates the hair, *fleshing*, the residue of subcutaneous fat known in the trade as 'flesh.' *Splitting* separates the layers of the skin while *pickling* opens its pores, removing the residues of lime. The phase of *tanning* proper, through the application of chromium salt, puts a complete halt to the process of decomposition. Then comes *selection*: the proportion of the material rejected is very high, with only 30 to 40 per cent of a batch being suitable for the best leather. Hides of inferior quality are used for applica-

Poppy: a precise reference to the history of Poltrona Frau, to the classicism of the form of its upholstered furniture. In the background, a model in London wearing a dress by John Bates, famous stylist of the seventies.

tions less demanding than our own. However, other imperfections may come to light at the end of the process: for instance the animal, when alive, always lies down on the same side, whether it is out to pasture or in its stall. Consequently, only one part of the hide is subject to wear. In addition, not all parts have the same degree of elasticity: the rump is much stiffer than the ventral zone. *Shaving* brings the leather to the desired thickness, but *re-tanning* gives it back the softness and naturalness that it had lost in the *chrome-tanning* process. Lastly comes the *dyeing* phase, carried out in casks where the aniline dye is allowed to soak right through the leather. The treatment makes it more resistant to scratching and prevents the phenomenon of peeling, typical of the samples we examined which had bare patches on the arms and other parts subject to wear. No scratching of our leather can cause it to deteriorate. *Pre-drying*, *air drying*, *reconditioning* with a layer of damp sawdust and *drying* on the frame are technical processes designed to give the product particular qualities. *Staking* is the operation carried out to detach fibers and results in a further softening of the leather. *Trimming* and *edging* eliminate the outer parts, which would not be used in our sort of production anyway. *Finishing* by spraying with resin increases the resistance to wear, light, staining and so on. Before the *measuring*, which is done with electronic instruments and is expressed in square meters, the pores of the leather are evened out by hot *ironing* and *pressing*. The whole of this ordeal is required to attain the best result: the finest leather. The procedure is to some extent related, though more complicated and technologically advanced, to the one described by Tommaso Garzoni in his *Piazza universale di tutte le professioni del mondo*. Yet while vegetable hair, cotton wadding, jute straps, the framework of artificially-seasoned beech wood, biconical springs and goose down are all elements in

Petronio, 1976, designed
by Tito Agnoli.
The high back, divided into
a continuous triple cushioning...
responds to ergonomic criteria
that ensure a correct and comfortable
posture.
On facing page, Armando Testa,
The Armchair, 1978.

the structure of an armchair or couch, it is the leather, perfectly tanned and beautiful in its new and sensual colors, that designs and molds its forms. That is how Luigi Massoni and I saw it. Within a short period of time we managed to rework a small collection of pieces, restoring a sense of authenticity to them in full. And while we had not broken the thread of continuity, it was now possible to forge ahead, to think about new designs, which would in any case benefit from previous experience. We had developed the grip necessary to move forward, having averted the risk of Poltrona Frau losing its identity. But we did not brag about our achievement: condition attained, period. Identity and continual updating of identity. This is the message that we wanted to get across, and it is one that I think is still conveyed by Poltrona Frau products today."

As individual, complete expressions, Lullaby, Dilly Dally and Criss Cross did not constitute furnishing accessories in matching style but were pieces of furniture in their own right, like the armchairs and couches, which could be located anywhere in the home: this was the prime characteristic of the Poltrona Frau product and Luigi Massoni underlined this through their innovative forms. No small innovation, this, but one that helped to put across the idea of the house not as a fixed backdrop for the activities of daily life, but as a space in which to live according to need. Thus the bed was no longer just a place for sleeping: Lullaby was what Massoni called it ironically, spurning the usual run of names. Round in shape and rotating through 360 degrees, it resembled a wheel that could be used to put the most inventive ideas in the *Kamasutra* into practice. It suggested the kind of transgression that Gabriele D'Annunzio (1863–1938) had already proposed for the armchair in *L'innocente* (published in English as *The Intruder*). "As it was wide and low she, who was slim, made room for me at her side and clung to me trembling. With one hand she took the hem of her cloak and covered me. It was as if we were in a bed, embracing breast to breast, our breath mingling."

Yet the armchair was still the prime symbol of the identity that the father bequeathed to his son. "A timid youth with lyrical possibilities," wrote Camillo Sbarbaro (1888–1967) in the fifth of his *Scampoli*, "his father was called Teodoro, just as the grandson would be called; he, Michele, as had been his grandfather's name. His father refused to let sunlight into the house. As long as his father lived, the son hated the armchair of faded and worn leather. He ridiculed the grandfather clock with its exposed weights that could be stopped just by blowing on it. Occasionally he would throw open a window, irritating the old man. But when his father died everything in the house became sacred. The son no longer dared to open the window now that his father was no longer there to slam it shut again. The idea of getting rid of the clock, now that his father was no longer there to defend it, seemed like sacrilege. And so the dead man succeeded in keeping everything as he had left it. And the house began to work its wiles on the son. Everything invited the living to take the place of the absent. The empty armchair was a reproach. One day he sat on it and found it comfortable. When the subscription to the newspaper of which the dead man was fond ran out, the son just had it renewed. And so the paper continued to be delivered in the deceased's name. In time the son took to wife the girl who his father had praised so many times: the one his father would have married himself. Little by little there was nothing left in the old house to show that Teodoro B. was no longer among the living. As the years went by the son even adopted the dead man's manner of speech. 'He's just like the dear departed,' people used to say. Thus Teodoro B. lived another time in this world."

The domineering father: paternal authority. In 1969 Umberto Eco examined the symbol of paternal authority in Gal's satirical cartoons in his preface to the review of the artist's work entitled *I boss media*. "Gal, for instance, proceeds by metonymies, naming an object through another to which it is related (such as container for content, or cause for effect). Except that, unlike the mechanism of the classical figure of speech, which works through replacement (and requires an effort of interpretation to trace what is named from the name), Gal prefers, owing to his concern for didactics and desire for satirical impact, to leave both terms of the relationship present. There is a relationship between the armchair, symbol of paternal authority, and the newspaper *Il Corriere della Sera*. But do we always remember it? Not always. Well, Gal constructs an armchair out of newspaper—the *Corriere* of course—and seats in it a gentleman in a stovepipe hat (antonomasia for the capitalist). Brutal? Brutal. Is it funny? It's funny, because in any case there is wit, baroque humor, mother of *Witz*, and therefore of the quip (which if it is concealed, unconscious, becomes a Freudian slip). But apart from the laugh (or the smile—a composed and sober reaction is allowed), what is left? A conceptualizable—and memorable—relationship. A didactic message about political judgment."

Yet it is still an armchair, in the first place symbol of comfort, *par excellence*. In its traditional form, however, the arms stick out, swollen and soft curves, protruding outward from the seat. Why such an encumbrance? They even stop you putting two or more armchairs or couches together, as Sergio Mazza and Giuliana Gramigna observed. If however, the arms too are a symbol of the softness of the seat, then why not turn them inward. That way they will accentuate the sense of comfort, even in visual terms, as well as making it easier to create a setting for conversation when needed.

"Our friend Luigi Massoni suggested to Franco Moschini that he ask us whether we would be interested in collaborating with Poltrona Frau. We accepted, believing that the conditions existed for us to express our own conception of design within the ambit of a culture of production, and the most tried and tested at that." In the preface to *Sergio Mazza e Giuliana Gramigna. Quarant'anni di professione*, Giuseppe Chigiotti notes: "Their approach to the profession is shaped by a strong belief in modernization, seeing rationalism and the Modern Movement as a utopian moment of great value that they have never disavowed. This is the way in which they have tackled design. Or rather, the design of furnishings… Sergio Mazza and Giuliana Gramigna's design is linked to architecture, like almost all Italian design: they see it as an offshoot of architectural culture. For conceptually it shares the same cultural aspirations that determine the currents and expressions of architecture. So it is that many objects,

Petronio can be traced back to the attitude to design current in the years when Italian design was at its peak, to a careful reformulation of the classical conception of the chair. Brigitte Bardot, a prominent campaigner in the first battles for animal's rights in 1975.

created for one kind of architecture, have gone on to be produced for other kinds... This way of working is typical of the architectural profession, at least in Italy. A *modus operandi* that had been defined at the very dawn of modernity. To such an extent that it troubled both Alberti and Ponti, and even Aldo Rossi. Architects and artists who have based their design on an all-embracing tendency. With the idea of making the world of design fit in with their own aesthetic vision and their own conception of creativity. Bringing works of architecture and objects under the umbrella of the same principles, in a vision that is summed up in the definition already provided by Ernesto Rogers. That an architect, faced with the possibilities of intervention, restricts them to a sphere extending from the spoon to the city."

And so Sergio Mazza and Giuliana Gramigna's design Smoking was taken up by Frau and put into production in 1970. "Smoking was our response," continues Giuliana Gramigna, "to the intention of maintaining the characteristics of the leather armchair: soft and comfortable. An ergonomically correct chair, but one that could be combined with others to make the best use of space. The idea of turning the curve of the arm inward and of extending the sides all the way down to the ground allowed us to define the form. The Smoking project was the only occasion on which we collaborated with Poltrona Frau, but for us it was an interesting and rewarding experience. In those years, in fact, we were designing for Artemide, working on the use of plastic and resins in furnishing, and we were dealing with the newest materials and technologies. We were well aware that only the design could justify their use: it was certainly not a question of following a fashion. Well, coming into contact, at the same time, with the distinctly traditional world of Poltrona Frau, in both its materials and its modes of production, we tried to capture the essence of its identity by creating Smoking: absolutely Frau, but in tune with our own understanding of design. No longer the upholsterer's arm-

chair, as Zanuso had already affirmed with Lady. So we thought, the cushioning is an added part, in four pieces: the two sides, the back and the seat, made individually by the most traditional methods and with the most traditional materials and then brought together to define the form of the armchair. However, the individual pieces, and as a consequence the armchair, were examples of a proven and perfected culture of production and testified to its fascination."

Massoni had also turned his attention to newer materials and technologies while he was working with Frau. "For Fratelli Guzzini," notes Anty Pansera, "for instance (and then for Rede as well) he tackled the theme of the plate, the container (in Homeforme), the glass... For Harvey Guzzini, now Guzzini Illuminazione, run by Adolfo, he designed a series of hanging and table lamps from the mid-sixties onward, seeking to identify the form that most suited the technologies involved... From 1967 onward, in addition, he coordinated the design of the DH brand, Design House (also part of Guzzini)—working alongside Adolfo and bringing in numerous other product and visual designers of great distinction, from Gio Ponti to Rodolfo Bonetto and from Cesare Casati to Tomoko Ponzio, Fabio Lenci, Ennio Lucini and Mimmo Castellano."

Certainly the majority of manufacturers had abandoned the materials and methods peculiar to the tradition of upholstered furniture: shaped polyurethanes were used to cover frames and provide padding, and covering was reduced to a

simple job of tailoring. The result was a line of production intended, as people used to say at that time, for the first home, that of the newlyweds who didn't have too much to spend. In his novel entitled *L'integrazione*, Luciano Bianciardi (1922–72) describes its furnishings in the voice of an "up-and-coming executive" returning home in the evening. "I get home tired but satisfied. We have a well-furnished and comfortable little apartment: it's the home of an up-and-coming executive, Marisa says. An ample couch in foam rubber and burnished metal in the living room, and the bookcase has movable elements, not set against the wall but strung between floor and ceiling. Thus it also serves to divide up the space, to separate the dining area from the sitting and reading area. We also have two or three antique pieces, not isolated and so-to-speak excluded from the rest of the house, but inserted into it, integrated with all that is modern in it. Lots of records, and good ones: Vivaldi of course and Bach, but spirituals too, which Marisa is very fond of, and the modern French songs of Georges Brassens, which I like. There's one really pretty one, the one about Marinette, in which every verse finishes with the words 'J'avais l'air d'un con, ma mère,' which means, 'What an idiot I seemed, mother,' but sounds much better in French.

Marisa has scattered ashtrays all over the place, of different shapes and sizes: made of pottery, glass, even wire, in the shape of a cat with a bow tie and a tray of hammered copper… I have been able to furnish the house so well and comfortably thanks to the help that my in-laws have given me: good, sensible people. I've signed forty promissory notes of twenty-five thousand each, and I'm paying them off month by month. For the moment we have no intention of bringing children into the world, but Marisa has promised me that as soon as they give her a contract, at the agency where she works, she'll let herself get pregnant. For the time being I have to be very careful, on Saturdays… And finally on Saturday evening we get home, at eleven… I take a bath, while Marisa takes out our poodle, called Guido, and lets him do

his business in the dirt road that is right under our house. When she comes back up I'm already in bed, and for a good half-hour, we forget about work, bills and worries, and are really there for each other. I sure hope that the agency gives her that blessed contract soon."

If we consider the description of the living space in Luciano Bianciardi's beautiful picture of people's lives, we notice that he does not mention the shape of the couch, but the fact that it is made of foam rubber, a new material. In those years, in fact, the emphasis was placed on the materials, independently of whether the design justified their use. This is why, when Roberto Canziani, at the head of Poltrona Frau at the time, gave in to pressure from Pirelli, which wanted to obtain the prestigious endorsement of the Turin brand for its foam rubber, and replaced traditional materials with the new one, he seriously compromised the company's image. On the contrary, Franco Moschini, even though he knew he was swimming against the tide, was to reject any change in Poltrona Frau's identity: his choice was, therefore, a reasoned and pragmatic one.

It was quite a different matter for the companies set up after the war which, thanks to the advent of new materials and technologies, came to dominate the wider market. However, they had to compete with one another over price, when the quality of their product was, in the majority of cases, more or less the same. So was the form, as they used the models that were most widely imitated and easiest to imitate. Apart from a few, which could be counted on the fingers of one hand, which relied from the outset on the added value of design. Even these could boast no difference in their culture of production. Of these few, Arflex, in collaboration with Marco Zanuso, made the best use of the new resources: foam rubber and then polyurethane. Within this narrow field, however, differences of design soon came to signify a battle of designers or of designer furniture: on the one hand standardized products, in which the models were copies of copies, on the other the rarefied, sophisticated market of furniture designed by well-known figures. Poltrona Frau kept away from both of these extremes, committing itself instead to maintaining its own culture, in a sort of self-conditioning that allowed it to avoid getting caught up in the price war or the battle of designers. At a time when the "made in Italy" label was represented at an international level and in the most varied

Billiard table covered entirely with leather, designed by Mario Bellini, 1982. On facing page, the three heroines of the American television series *Charlie's Angels*, a cult in those years, and a *haute couture* design by Roberto Capucci.

areas of the market by precisely those manufacturers whose selling point was design.

In my *Pininfarina. Identity of a Design*, I described the Cisitalia 202 of 1947, by the Turinese entrepreneur of design Pinin Farina, now in the MoMA in New York, as an archetype of the automobile: "Undoubtedly critics all over the world were asking themselves, and are still wondering today, about the reasons for the symbolic significance of the 202 sedan… Pinin himself comments: 'I had arrived at a point in the work where what counted was neither the technical know-how nor the pure form, but being able to put them together, without effort or at least without revealing the effort.'" And on the subject of the Aurelia B24 of 1954 and

the Giulietta Spider of 1955, the custom-built cars that put into mass production and invented the category of the fast touring car: "Pinin sowed the seed, in 1954, of a new conception of the automobile body. He feared that taking the process of rounding to an extreme would result in a weakening of the lines and set out to restore the balance. The shell of the B24 is supported by very sturdy flanges that do not detract from the plasticity of the design but enhance it. And if this V-6 with a cylinder capacity of 2451 cc looks like it is in movement even when standing still, this is due to the fact that its appearance is a perfect expression of the designer's intentions. The same intentions that would lead to the creation of the Giulietta Spider the following year." Franco Moschini decided even then that the way to demonstrate

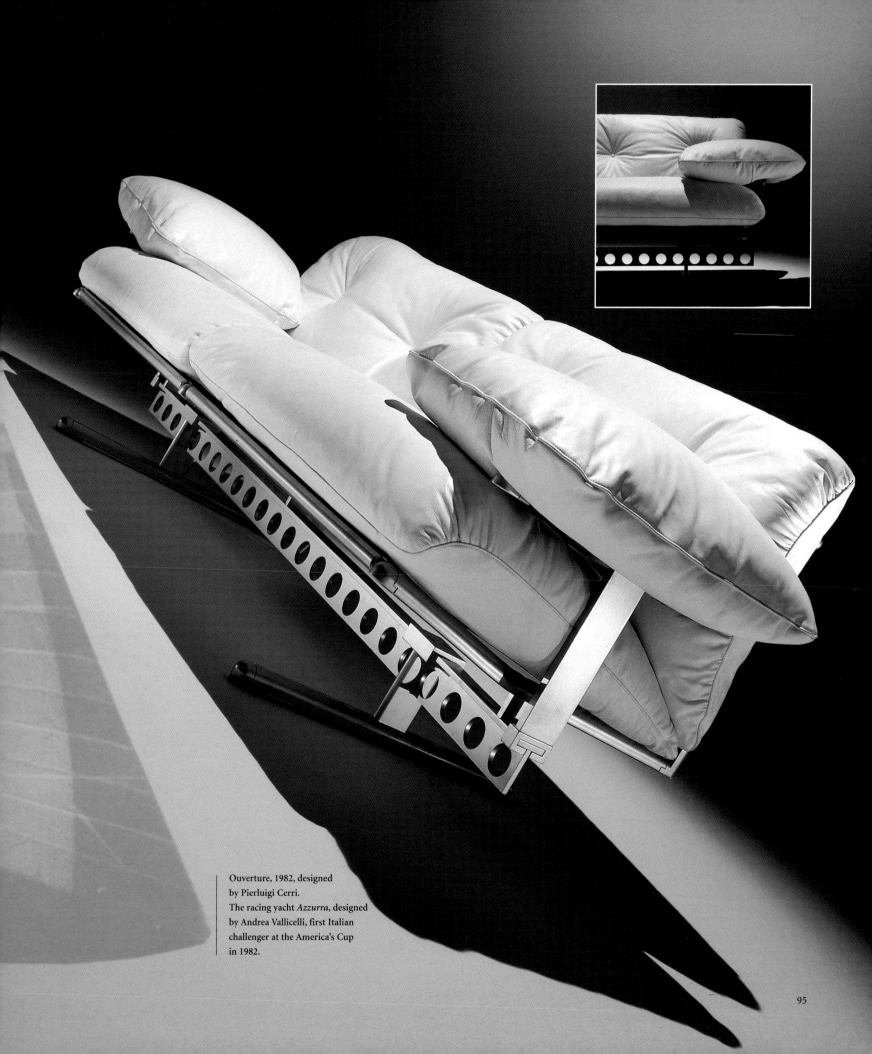

Ouverture, 1982, designed
by Pierluigi Cerri.
The racing yacht *Azzurra*, designed
by Andrea Vallicelli, first Italian
challenger at the America's Cup
in 1982.

95

In Pierluigi Cerri's Ouverture, a solid base acts as a counterpoint to the theme of the seats freely expressed in the cadence of the soft cushions in high-quality leather.

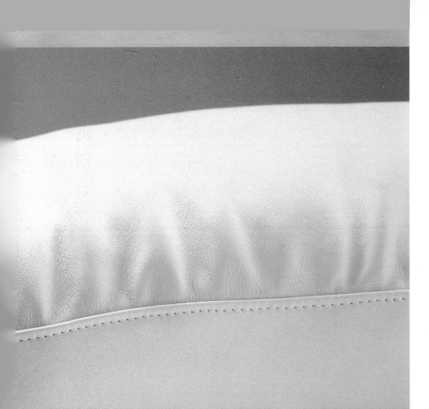

Frau culture was to emphasize its different functions in relation to different settings: the user would find that its appeal and quality remained the same not just in the home, but also in the office, the theater and the most desirable of vehicles and would recognize Poltrona Frau as author of the various proposals, of an exclusive way of living.

"I had already designed armchairs and couches for Cinova," recalls Tito Agnoli, "and the 9000 series for Arflex, which broke the record for production. My knowledge of the sector was limited to foams, polyurethanes and metal frames that they covered. So I asked Franco Moschini if I could spend a few days in the factory before accepting his proposal of collaboration. I wanted to gain a thorough understanding of the dynamics of production, which were substantially different from my previous experiences. The first thing that struck me was the central part played by the human being: as in the

glass factories on Murano, the master craftsmen all had a significant role in the definition of the product. Yet no one plays second fiddle in this fascinating merry-go-round. Everyone contributes to the final result and they all seem to want to communicate their individual espousal of this approach to the work. I liked the atmosphere, the commitment of all the workers. This helped me to understand what part I could play in the process. I had to immerse myself in the traditional culture, in all its sophistication and refinement, and design models that would bear witness to its rarity and value." In his monograph on Tito Agnoli, Flavio Conti says: "The fact is that he revived the figure of the old-time craftsman and made it relevant to the present situation. He is, first and last, a craftsman of design... He works 'in the

shop,' i.e. at the companies with which he collaborates, developing the form not from an abstract idea but directly out of the effort of construction. With an attitude like this it is only natural that he finds himself most at ease when working with craft-based companies, where the design has to make the most of the material and of the manual skill of the workers." Poppy of 1975 and Petronio of 1976 were Agnoli's first proposals in tune with the Frau culture of production. According to the presentation of the Poppy model: "The cushion of the seat extends without a break into the protruding arm and determines the formal characteristics of the couch. It is made particularly comfortable by the large amount of down used and the fact that the back is available in two different heights. An internal compartmentalization of the cushioning, a constant feature of Frau production, means that the down is held in place by partitions." And here

Agnoli seems to have wanted to get his hand in with the materials and modes of production through a precise reference to the history of Poltrona Frau, to the classical quality of its upholstered furniture, so like that of the armchair in the story *I ranoni* by Filippo de Pisis (1896–1956), published in *La città dalle cento meraviglie.* "I remember (oh, blessed times that perhaps did not seem as blessed to me as the present, as I did not then know how to create a sense of bliss for myself in the way that I do now), I remember on certain afternoons when I was wandering around the stinking retteries in the lowlands, oppressed by the heat, seeing certain peaceful and Socratic frogs lurking on a round white stone dried by the sun and covered with white clay, with their front legs bowed, their short webbed toes spread wide and their round and bulging eyes flecked with gold, and their spotted skin, gleaming in the sun. If I bend over my table, crouched in the big

Lancia Thema 8:32, 1982.
The year 1982 marked the birth
of Frau Car, although it did not
become a proper division until 1984.
On facing page, detail of the dashboard
and the front seats.

armchair, amidst the books scattered all over the place and stretch out my small, white palms on the wooden surface, I greatly enjoy the idea of being a frog puffed up with happiness, with a white shirtfront and a double chin."

Thus Poppy was the model of transition, still linked to the traditional image of the "big armchair," when Agnoli was already designing combinations of individual seats: Petronio. It was described in the presentation as follows: "Its structural and formal characteristics can be traced back to the attitude to design current in the years when Italian design was at its peak, to a careful reformulation of the classical conception of the chair, an attitude that developed in opposition to tendencies of a more radical and experimental nature. In Petronio, the high back, divided into a continuous triple cushioning (seat, kidney rest and backrest), supported by the gently inclined framework, responds to ergonomic criteria that ensure a correct and comfortable posture. It is covered with high-quality leather and a number of specially designed elements within the system allow it to be combined in infinite ways." However, Petronio was a synonym for the combination alone so that the armchair was a finished piece that went to make up the mosaic and in no way undermined the distinctive guarantees and appeal of the Frau product.

"I have always looked," comments Tito Agnoli, "at function first, and then form. And in this case I wanted to distinguish two functions, one single, the armchair, the other multiple, the sectional system. And if the latter is an extension of the former, then it is all the more true that it is shaped by the form of the individual piece. In Poltrona Frau I found the best partner for a demonstration of the theorem."

For, as Angelo Cortesi writes in *Letteratura e scienza, le poetiche del design*: "The rationalist current works in close con-

The steering wheel in the magical
hands of the upholsterer.
On facing page, details of the interiors
that reveal the softness and quality
of Poltrona Frau leather.

D.I.T.
LIBRARY
MOUNTJOY SQ.

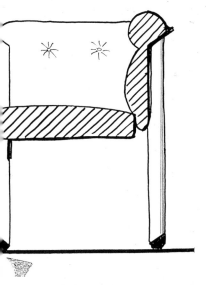

nection with the rules of the Modern Movement, of the Bauhaus and the Hochschule in Ulm, and therefore seeks to express the principles of form follows function with the greatest consistency possible. The above principles are naturally filtered through the great formal sensibility of the Italian figurative tradition. Some of the greatest Italian designers belong to this current: M. Bellini, R. Bonetto, M. Zanuso, G. Giugiaro, Design Group Italia, A. van Onck, G. Frattini, C. Bartoli, T. Agnoli, G. Stoppino, B. Gecchelin, Cini Boeri, A. Castelli Ferrieri, P. Spadolini, G. Decursu. Mario Bellini says that 'The designer is only one part of design; design is only one part of industrial planning; industrial planning is a phase in the continuous process of social planning.

Interlude, 1983, designed by Marco Zanuso. The *master* had started to show an interest in those forms of craftsmanship that were closest to the evolution of the technological process. This was what brought him to Poltrona Frau.

Only after all this has been made clear do I believe that it is possible to claim that the plan has an emergent value, and above all a value as the fundamental condition of any form of intelligent life. No civilization, not even those that have differed most greatly from our own, has been able not merely to grow but even to develop or survive without a plan.'"

In *Il disegno del prodotto industriale: Italia 1860-1980*, Giampiero Bosoni says of Mario Bellini: "Bellini based his own creative process on the confidence that he would be able to work out an authentically integral procedure of design for the construction of the industrial object. In a

turned to Mario Bellini in 1982 for the design of a classic object of leisure, the billiard table, sure that we could rely on his distinct flair for experimentation. Given a tried and tested technical structure, and therefore an already fully resolved function, we wanted to find a form better suited to its insertion in a domestic setting. Of course, this was no easy task, in the absence of precedents. This is perhaps what induced Bellini to take on the task of designing a covering for the structure that Hermelin supplied us. Thus we produced a billiard table of great appeal, covered entirely with leather, with twelve supports that echoed the squaring of the top and

Interlude, starring on the set
of the television program *Mai dire mai*.
On facing page, detail of the armchair
showing the contrast between
the upholstered and structural parts.

way Bellini was to the seventies what Zanuso had been for the previous generation. The designer certainly no longer saw the industrial world as a marvelous discovery but as a natural component, even when he seemed to be involved more closely, experimenting in a different way, with the world of meaningful plasticity. Bellini seems to have looked for the marvelous elsewhere: in experimental curiosity, in the mimicry of organic processes of formation apparently so remote from his own creative will." Franco Moschini recalls: "Still within the perspective of a philosophy aimed at making the Frau mode of living recognizable everywhere, we

in eleven different colors. The playing surface was covered with green or gunmetal baize and it had a full set of accessories, including ten normal cues and two long ones, bridges, an electronic timer and balls. We had succeeded in turning the billiard table into a timeless, Frau piece of furniture. In fact leather has always been the material best suited to the configuration of the object."

The year 1982 marked the birth of Frau Car, although it did not become a proper division until 1984. And it was certainly no coincidence that the project involved a collaboration with Lancia given that, way back in the twenties, Renzo Frau

Images from the early eighties:
Keith Haring, *Untitled*, 1984,
Stuttgart, Kaess Weiss Gallery.
Rainbow personal computer, 1984.
On facing page, the aggressive look
of a London punk.

used to supply Vincenzo Lancia with refined upholstery for the Turin constructor's most demanding customers. The Thema 8:32, with a Ferrari engine, was the true heir of those legendary automobiles, taking up the thread of continuity. It also represented a further step in the diversification of settings for Frau. Franco Moschini was convinced that the future of the automobile would be dependent on the safety and comfort offered by the interior of individual vehicles. If the criteria on which the former were based would be developed through research, then those of the latter would have to keep abreast with their evolution. "And safety is precisely the objective that, ever since the sixties," I observed in *Pininfarina. Identity of a Design*, "has been pursued by Pininfarina and that best defines its ecology of automobile design. The reconciliation of technology and aesthetics is nevertheless always carried out in relation to the idea that it is the human being who uses the car and not the car that uses the human being. 'At the beginning of the twentieth century,' explains Sergio, 'the automobile was god and the human was at the service of the automobile god. Not any more. Everything is dependent on the human being: I brake and the servo brake acts for me. There are even quiet Ferraris,

with automatic transmission. I remember that Enzo Ferrari wanted his cars to have light flywheels, and this made it difficult to change gear. Not on a whim, but to underline the lightness of the vehicle. So the future has more automobiles in store for us. Standards of living are going to rise. We shall all be richer and the very rich will be poorer. This is why the automobile will also have the job of making up for all the negative effects that it has had over the course of its history. So the problems of safety and pollution will be solved, but the designer can only make a contribution to this. The whole of society will have to tackle the problem of the automobile, which involves city planning and the road system. However, it will increasingly be the task of the designer to give a shape to technological progress, pursuing a synthesis of technology and aesthetics, with the result that niche products will preserve the memory of historic changes while the car, in general, will just be the most advanced means of transport. My father always believed that our small company should perform the function of a catalyst for the rest of the automobile market. This is even more true today, when the niche product will have the job of bringing back under human control just those technologies that are threatening to escape from it. This is the sense of our technical and aesthetic research into the automobile, now as in the past, of our production: the continual and thorough updating of the significance of this catalytic function.'"

Renzo Frau had also encountered Vincenzo Lancia and Pinin Farina on the road. Franco Moschini now set out to follow his example by placing Frau Car at the service of the niche product, of that product that, as Sergio Pininfarina put it "will have the job of bringing back under human control just those technologies that are threatening to escape from it." As the presentation of the Thema 8:32 "Interior in Frau Leather" declared: "A few basic values have recurred constantly in the history of Poltrona Frau. Craftsmanship, for example, understood as know-how passed down from master to pupil and becoming tradition. And the choice of materials, always natural and carefully selected. Or the exclusive treatment of the leather, subjected to highly sophisticated processes to ensure that its characteristics remain constant over time... Our experience in the manufacture of armchairs and couches by means of ancient techniques allows us to apply the same philosophy to the upholstery of cars, using exclusively manual techniques and special methods of sewing. Operating on the basis of these rigorous methodologies, it has been possible to achieve an ideal combination of anticipation of the future (original mechanical solutions, innovative materials, sophisticated technologies) and traditional techniques." These are features of great significance: the meaning of craftsmanship lies in the body of

The Sala Frau at Spoleto, 1984.
The Poltrona Frau contract
commenced with the restoration
and fitting out of the former parish
hall of the church of San Gregoriuccio
alla Sinagoga at Spoleto, to a design
by the architect Paolo Rosmini.

character and special treatment means that its transpiration varies with the seasons: soft and yielding in the winter, cool and airy in the summer. Moreover, the hides used for the upholstery of cars have to pass a series of severe tests, providing additional guarantees."

Thus the guarantee offered was extended from one of greater comfort to one of greater safety. "With the 8:32 and its Ferrari engine, eight cylinders, four valves per cylinder, a niche automobile with respect to the Thema 2000 of the normal Lancia production," recalls Franco Moschini, "we were working for the first time as contractors, in close collaboration with the Styling Center of the Turin manufacturer. And we realized that the rules of the game were highly favorable to us, a quite different situation from the supply of armchairs to private customers or public bodies. The client of the Car Division has a precise specification that it wants respected, as its image is involved. So it is our task to achieve a result that, while respecting the rules imposed by the function, will enhance both the comfort and the safety of the design. Here the value of our stock of know-how, of our craftsmanship, is revealed not just in the upholstery of the seats, but also in the covering of the instrument panel and dashboard. In fact we rejected the body maker's custom of gluing the leather onto a metal backing, consisting of those parts of the interior of the vehicle that need to be lined, and replaced with the upholsterer's practice of stretching and punching. And if we note

knowledge which masters pass down to their pupils and which establishes a dialogue with the most sophisticated technology. And, since ancient times, this dialogue has not threatened a loss of identity but, if anything, has helped to enrich it. In this sense Poltrona Frau had no compunction in declaring, even in its Car Division, that its predilection for leather "stems from several fundamental characteristics of the material. Starting with the fact that leather remains unchanged over time and that its quality—first-rate and therefore particularly prized—is combined with a highly sophisticated treatment in the tanning and dyeing phases. Processes that ensure on the one hand a very soft finish and on the other that the color is not confined to the surface but penetrates right through the material, making it impervious to scratches." Thus the Frau heritage of know-how served as a guarantee for the client, Lancia.

"The treatments and procedures used by Frau bring out aspects of great value in the material, such as its aesthetic quality, from the surface that is always pleasant to the touch to the new range of colors. Or other aspects linked to practicality and resistance. The leather does not stain and dirt can be removed with nothing more than water and mild soap. It also breathes and does not absorb odors, maintaining the maximum of hygiene. In addition to improving with age, the leather is suited to all kinds of weather. In fact its natural

Madonna, rising star of the eighties: on the cover of her first album and with Rosanna Arquette in Susan Seidelman's movie *Desperately Seeking Susan*, 1985. Antropovarius, 1985, designed by Ferdinand Alexander Porsche.

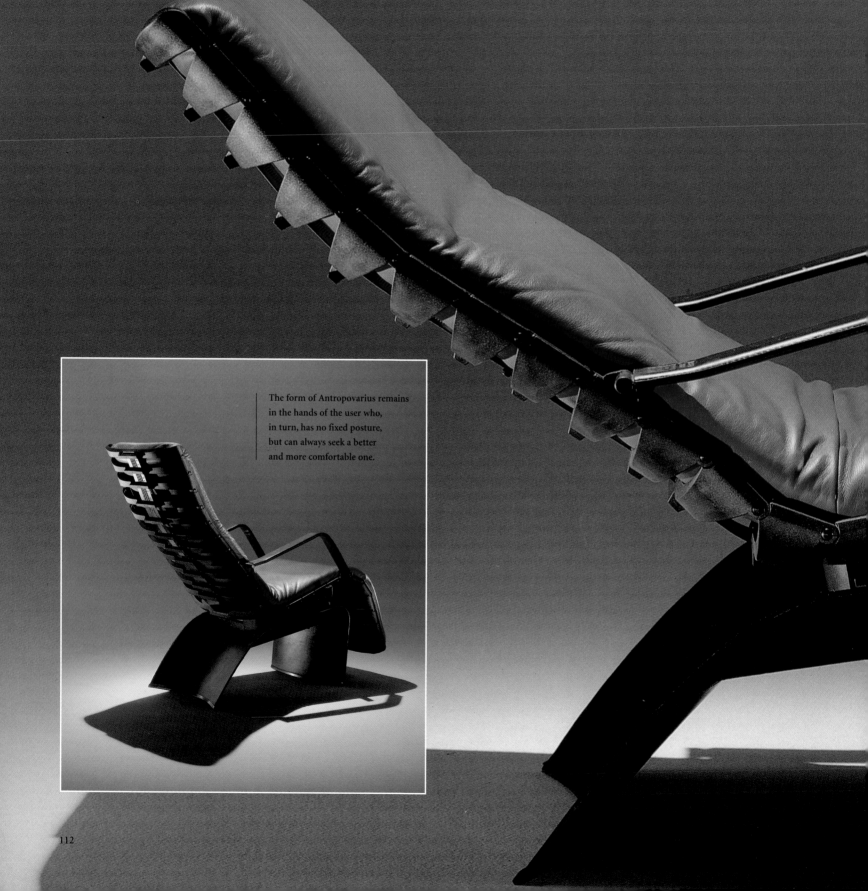

The form of Antropovarius remains
in the hands of the user who,
in turn, has no fixed posture,
but can always seek a better
and more comfortable one.

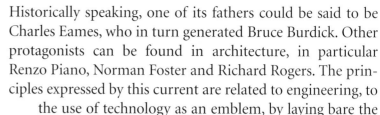

Historically speaking, one of its fathers could be said to be Charles Eames, who in turn generated Bruce Burdick. Other protagonists can be found in architecture, in particular Renzo Piano, Norman Foster and Richard Rogers. The principles expressed by this current are related to engineering, to the use of technology as an emblem, by laying bare the structure of a building or a product. The current tends to see technology as being naturally expressive, as if it had no need of interpretation. The end result often attains a high degree of expressiveness. The exponents of this current in Italy are R. Sapper, G. Piretti, A. Meda, P. Rizzato, C. Forcolini, Pallucco, P. Cerri and P. Castiglioni. Richard Sapper says: 'So, now I know why I always feel reluctant to explain my work when someone asks me to. There is nothing to explain. When you're designing you don't think in words, but in three-dimensional, colored, self-

that automobile manufacturers are placing even more emphasis on the quality of the vehicle's interior today, in relation of course to the category to which it belongs, then we can say that they are increasingly concerned with ensuring the safety and quality of the upholstery. The 8:32 gave us the opportunity to plan the future of our Car Division, making us feel that we had a role to play in the evolution of the automobile."

In that year of 1982 Poltrona Frau not only launched Mario Bellini's billiard table and its Car Division with the Thema 8:32, but also Pierluigi Cerri's Ouverture, which is still a classic example of the research carried out by the company into different technologies. "The high-tech style," observes Angelo Cortesi, "has no precedents in Italian design.

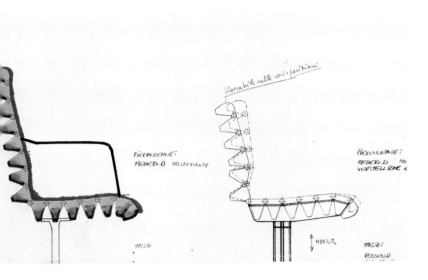

propelled images, that touch one another, making a noise sometimes. They can even get hot and burn you. Thus the materials are involved, the sensations of surfaces, vapors, fire, and in the end we are going to eat what they contain. I hope it's good.'"

So Ouverture has a sense of opening, of going beyond, especially when seen in relation to musical notation: since the nineteenth century, the overture has been the introduction to the work itself, a free anticipation of the themes that will be developed as it unfolds. In Pierluigi Cerri's Ouverture, a solid base acts as a counterpoint to the theme of the seats freely expressed in the cadence of the soft cushions in high-quality leather. Thanks to the continuous system of support, the seats declare themselves to be the essence of comfort. Truly an advance, a step forward in the organization of living, especially when compared with the furniture of the past, individual presences like the ones described by James Joyce in *Ulysses*: "Two chairs had been moved from right and left of the ingleside [...]. One: a squat stuffed easychair with stout arms extended and back slanted to the rere, which, repelled in recoil, had then upturned an irregular fringe of a rectangular rug and now displayed on its amply upholstered seat a centralized diffusing and diminishing discoloration. The other: a slender splayfoot chair of glossy cane curves [...]. What significances attached to these two chairs? Significances of similitude, of posture, of symbolism, of circumstantial evidence, of testimonial supermanence." Emblematic individual configurations characterize the living space, whereas Ouverture is a suggestion of the configuration, not a definition of it: the counterpoint sustains the song. According to the presentation: "The structure is a steel

truss, while cushions, seat, back and arms are padded with goose down."

With Ouverture, Poltrona Frau took on different technologies and construction materials. "We are convinced," comments Franco Moschini, "that the right thing for us is to produce only those designs in which we can recognize ourselves and in which, as a consequence, it is always possible to recognize the contribution of our know-how, our craftsmanship. In this way we are enriched in the process, which constitutes a new experience. Ouverture tackled themes of the work that we are still exploring today. And they can be summed up in the correct and well-founded use of those technologies and materials that are best suited to our curiosity as craftsmen. In this way, it is always we who choose, never the other way round. And the affirmation of the ethical viewpoint lends meaning to the effort, translating it into a guarantee: we attach great importance to the assertion that we believe in the possibility of putting the evolution of technology back in touch with the needs of human beings."

Pierluigi Cerri's Ouverture, which declared itself the essence of comfort, was followed in 1983 by Marco Zanuso's Interlude, designed by the man whom all Italian designers acknowledge as their master. Referring to the feeling of unease experienced by Marco Zanuso over the more radical forms of design that emerged in those years, François

Details of the structure of Antropovarius. The keys provided in the Antropovarius structure are the means used to adjust it to the sitter's posture.

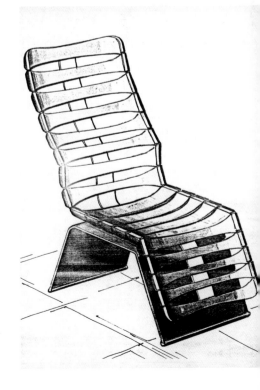

Burkhardt declares in his monograph devoted to the designer: "It is true that the concept of design defended by Marco Zanuso was quite the opposite of the one proposed by his younger colleagues gathered around Ettore Sottsass, Andrea Branzi and Alessandro Mendini. Zanuso followed attentively the development of these movements, yet found it difficult to sort out their more radical aspects: those of anti-industrialization and anti-technology, the artistic vision outside the professional context of design and the absence of the idea of the industrial object. For Zanuso the caricature of 'merchandise,' and therefore of the material content of the vocation of design for political and social reasons connected with the 'hopes' that were born around 1968 and that at first would find no outlet, constituted an insuperable gap. Yet the movement was to revolutionize the formal and methodological aspects of design and to propose industrial approaches oriented toward genres that had been marginalized for a long time, until a consensus with the manufacturers was reached in the early eighties. This rapprochement restored Zanuso's interest in the search for a new way of interpreting a production and distribution based on the small and medium run, with the revival of aspects of artisan production closely bound up with processes of advanced technological development."

With his Lady of 1951, Zanuso's prime concern had been not so much the form of the armchair as an attempt to introduce assembly-line methods, with the assembly of semifinished pieces, into the production of upholstered furniture. The justification for this lay in the need to make the best use of new technological resources in the manufacturing process. In the eighties, when furniture manufacturers began to place limits on mass production so as to diversify the range of articles on offer, Zanuso started to show an interest in those forms of craftsmanship that were closest to the evolution of the technological process. This was what brought him to Poltrona Frau.

"Interlude," comments Marco Zanuso, "reminds me of a story that I still like to tell today. In July 1983, Giampiero Pistacchi came to see me in my studio with the prototype of my armchair that was to be shown at the Salone del Mobile in September. We agreed to make a few modifications. He told me we should meet again before the end of the month, so that I could approve the final version. I had already packed my instruments and bags, ready to leave for the Greek island of Paxos where, ever since I bought a small plot of land with three ruined buildings and created a small vacation home for family use, I go for a long time every summer to recuperate. I told him: I have no intention of staying in Milan. He answered: I'll see you on Paxos. I really thought he was joking. But a week later, when I was already on the island, I see a powerful motorboat tying up in the little harbor, with Interlude lashed to its bows. We opened a magnum of champagne, right there on the wharf, to celebrate along with the crew of the motorboat the launch of the armchair that had made such a long trip to earn my approval. I had the chance to meet Giampiero Pistacchi again, at the time when Frau's seats were being delivered to the Piccolo Teatro in Milano. He came along this time too, though it wasn't July and, above all, the prototype didn't need modification. It was great to find the same sense of responsibility intact, twenty years later, in people who can still boast of their craftsmanship. I was sure that I could rely on Poltrona Frau when I asked Franco Moschini to take on the contract."

And twenty years earlier, Interlude itself had shown that Zanuso could be relied on to come up with an advanced technical solution that was fully in keeping with Poltrona Frau's stock of know-how, something that was made clear in the presentation of the chair: "The Interlude model, by Marco Zanuso, proposes a homogeneity of form and dimension between the arm and back elements that results in a particularly soft and comfortable chair. Aluminum plates covered with leather and with the internal structure made of wood constitute the supporting framework, while the seat with greek springs and the back serve to inflate the rubberized horsehair. The particularly supple form of this piece—armchair and two-seater couch—stems from the stuffing, arranged diagonally on slender legs of painted aluminum or chromed steel." In the description of the piece we find respect for the design, loving care and a painstaking search for the right solution. And these can be considered constant features of Frau's approach in all the different areas in which it operates.

The same can be said of the contract that arose out of the restoration and furnishing of the former parish hall of the church of San Gregoriuccio alla Sinagoga in Spoleto, in 1984. To a design by the architect Paolo Rosmini, the preexisting structures were renovated, the surviving traces of the fine architecture rendered visible and a theater was created: called the "Sala Frau," it was to become one of the venues for the Festival of Two Worlds. "This meant," recalls Moschini, "being able to inscribe the name Frau on the official list of one the most famous music festivals in the world. So it was an opportunity that could not be missed. These festivals have a long history behind them. The first was held in seventeenth-century England and from there they spread through Europe in the age of Romanticism, staged at concert halls in every country outside the opera season. Today very few of them are left on the calendar: two in Great Britain, Edinburgh and Glyndebourne; Bayreuth in Germany, devoted exclusively to Wagner; Salzburg in Austria, devoted largely to the music of Mozart; three in Italy: the Maggio Musicale in Florence, the Festival of Contemporary Music in Venice and, among the most prestigious, thanks to the untiring efforts of Giancarlo Menotti, Spoleto. In France there are still Aix-en-Provence and the Festival of Nations in Paris."

Much closer to the time of the first music festivals in England, Tommaso Garzoni da Bagnocavallo (1519–1589) dedicated discourse XLII of his *Piazza universale di tutte le professioni del mondo* to "Musicians, both singers and players" and defined the science, the art of making music. "This comprises (to put it simply) all the harmonies, and first the air, the tone with its varieties, the major and minor semitones, as well as the diesis, and then the unison, the ditone, the semiditone, the tritone, the diatessaron, the diapente, the major and minor hexachord. Which harmonies are known to the moderns by the names of major third, minor third, fifth and major and minor sixth; and these are called simple harmonies. After which come the compound ones, that is the

I Madrigali 4, 1987, designed by Fabio Lenci and Giovanna Talocci. On facing page, some Swatch models of 1987, a symbol of the eighties.

I Madrigali 4 are inspired
by the traditional form of the canopy
or four-poster bed, but gradually
incorporate other functions, taking
the contraption further and further
toward an exaltation of its playful
possibilities.

In 1987 Bertolucci's movie *Last Tango in Paris* returned to Italian movie screens, after being banned by the censors in 1976. In the picture, Maria Schneider and Marlon Brando. I Madrigali 4, with every part covered in magical, soft and sensual leather.

octave called diapason, the tenth, the twelfth, the tenth third, the tenth fifth, the tenth seventh, the ninth tenth, the twentieth, the second twentieth, and others *ad infinitum*, if only voice and sound could go on *ad infinitum*. They are followed by the three scales out of which each song is woven, i.e. the diatonic, the chromatic and the enharmonic. And then counterpoint; and after that the mode, the tempo and the prolation with their styles. And then the voice in singing: that of the tenor, the bass, the contralto, the contrabass; and the cantus fermus, the figured, the syncope, the pause, the sign and countersign, and singing in harmony with voices of several kinds: syneche, diastema, unison, conson, equison, emmeleia, acmeleia. And the notes with their values, i.e. maxima, long, breve, semibreve, minim, semiminim, chrome, semichrome and dots. And then full notes, hollow notes, ligatures, square and oblique notes, ascending and descending notes, perfect, altered and imperfect notes, of which things all music is filled from the beginning to the end." The words of Tommaso Garzoni reverberate and tumble, in themselves a rapid, effervescent and impetuous chromatic scale. However the science he is writing about is not the music with its crescendos and diminuendos; it is just the instrument used to create it. In fact, even though he knows the language, he is not capable of making music through the alchemy of words.

And so, to push the analogy further: the science called ergonomics is indeed an instrument, but the relationship of synergy between Poltrona Frau and Porsche was capable of translating the alchemy of its alphabet into music. The encounter between Poltrona Frau and the designer and eldest son of Ferry Porsche, known as Butzi, the creator of the body of the legendary 911, was certainly no accident. Franco Moschini was aware of the genetic inheritance of Porsche, knowing that Ferry had defined the identity of the 911 as follows. "Having opted for a very personal conception of the vehicle, characterized by an in-line six-cylinder, air-cooled engine, located at the rear, we certainly hadn't picked an easy road. We had to solve numerous problems without being able to benefit from the experience of other constructors. In the end events proved us right. The 911 turned out not only to be a sports car ideally suited for everyday use, but also the most versatile vehicle ever to have competed in rallies and on racetracks all over the world. Whether these were versions similar to the production model or modified in accordance with the current racing rules, the 911 has won practically every race for sports vehicles. It is as much at its

ease on the snow-covered roads of the Montecarlo Rally as on the desert trails of the Paris-Dakar, the twisting roads of the Targa Florio and the Daytona circuit, or the 24 Hours at Le Mans, all races that are now inscribed on its roll of honor." This is what Ferdinand Porsche had to say in the preface to Paul Frere's book *Porsche 911*. And in an article entitled "La Porsche evoluzione e design," published in *Abitare* no. 379, December 1998, I wrote: "The enthusiast has the impression that everything is justified in that gleaming aggregate of technology and form that is able to handle any road. Driving the 911 means becoming aware of the harmonious synthesis attained by its constructor, putting yourself at the keyboard of an organ and knowing that the organ has nothing in common with any other instrument that is more or less in tune. Rarely has a moving object achieved the integration of hardware and software to be found in the 911. And each time Porsche establishes the limits, only to attempt to overcome them the next time. This is the fundamental principle of Porsche's intelligent approach to production: only an object designed for mass production can be called a prototype for mass production."

Thus Porsche's DNA consists of a determination to marry technology and aesthetics, to pursue a synthesis. In this sense, the synergetic meeting of Poltrona Frau and Porsche is an expression of both bodies of knowledge, translated into the harmonic configuration of Antropovarius. "When Poltrona Frau got in touch with me to discuss the design of an advanced and special kind of armchair," declared Ferdinand Alexander Porsche in *Casa Oggi* (no. 159, 1987), "I did not hide my doubts and prejudices about the design of furniture, a sector that I have always considered extremely hackneyed." He was afraid that his partner might just add to a panorama already crowded with unjustified designs. "I had already done many designs in this field without ever realizing them, as there was always the risk of lapsing into banality. Designs commissioned by manufacturers all over the world come out of our studio, and it is our custom always to base the design of objects on thorough analysis and patient research. The reassurance given me by Poltrona Frau, that they wanted me to take a completely different approach from the practice current in the world of furnishing, was decidedly stimulating. In order to carry out such a project, out of the ordinary managerial skills and production facilities were required: producing an armchair that could really be adapted to any stature, when people display such a wide range of physiological variation, was not going to be an easy task, especially in view of the fact that I had to involve experts from various fields in the project, starting with that of ergonomics. I was struck by the fact that the people at Frau were not put off by these difficulties, and were not even bothered by my 'unconventional' attitude toward the tradition of the 'armchair,' in which I wanted to draw on our numerous earlier experiences, including those in the field of engineering, and to apply the concept of transfer (from one product to another, from one technology to another) that I had already tried out in other cases." This was a precise statement of method.

But the partner too, confident of its own methods, was not afraid of tackling the problem head on: so Poltrona Frau and Porsche realized Antropovarius together, in a fusion of technology and aesthetics, and went on to derive a whole range of furniture from it. Thus in that year of 1984, both were able to recognize themselves in the design that launched their synergetic collaboration, and they still do so today. "After the armchair for relaxation had been produced, the Antropovarius Office range was born, comprising the presidential chair (with a high back), the executive chair (with a back of medium height) and a small armchair for meetings. The principle governing its structure was based on the articulated and coordinated movement of seat and back, ensuring the maximum of comfort in the various positions in which it can be used. In addition to the ribbed structure, which permitted the maximum adaptability of the back to the body, other mechanisms made it possible to extend the seat and to adjust the height. For the Office model as well, the central theme of the research was: how to respond to the great diversity in people's sizes. The experience gained in the world of work through ergonomic research, as well as the more recent research carried out by the automobile and aerospace industries, was evaluated and integrated in a specific program of research conducted for Poltrona Frau by Heiner Bubb, a scientist working at the Institute of Ergonomics at the Technische Universität in Munich. He concluded his report as follows: 'On the basis of the data provided by the relevant literature, combined with that obtained through firsthand experience and taking all anthropometrical measurements into account, it is evident that the only way to obtain a correct seat is by providing for individual adaptation of the armchair.' Such adaptability was obtained through two different levels of adjustment: the first, which could be altered to suit the needs of the moment, involved the extension of the seat and the adjustment of the height;

the second, more personalized level, entailed altering the profile of the ribs to adapt it to the physique of the person who usually sat in it."

Thus the keys provided in the Antropovarius structure were the means used to adjust it to the sitter's posture. Hence the form of the armchair remained in the hands of the user and could be altered whenever necessary: the sitter does not have a fixed posture, but is always seeking a better and more comfortable one. And if the DNA of Porsche's approach to design, aimed at development of the synthesis between technology and aesthetics, is recognizable in the armchair, so is that of the studio's partner Poltrona Frau in its determination to bring it into production. Antropovarius is a timeless piece of furniture, as old as humanity, a classic amongst the most classic of armchairs: the fact that, even back in Renzo's time, leather armchair meant Frau Armchair was no mere play on words.

"However," comments Franco Moschini, "sticking to our objective of broadening the sense of Frau living space, in 1987 we decided to turn our attention once again to the sleeping area, the most private part of the home. We had already revolutionized its parameters with Luigi Massoni in 1968, at a time when it was seen as a place suited exclusively to period furniture. With Fabio Lenci and Giovanna Talocci, we produced a bed that was intended to be a summation of the most varied and seductive technological possibilities of the time."

By defining the bed as a "contraption on which one lies down unclothed to sleep" in his *Prontuario di vocaboli attenenti a parecchie arti, ad alcuni mestieri, a cose domestiche, e altre di uso comune*, Giacinto Carena (1778–1859) undoubtedly placed limits on its functions, while going on to specify the different types: "*Double Bed*, elliptical denomination of a bed for two, i.e. one that is wide enough for two people. *Twin Beds*, two small and identical beds that, if so desired, can be moved alongside by means of their castors, and used to make a double bed. *Cot, Crib, Pallet*, all names for beds of small size. *Canopy or Four-Poster Bed*, one with drapes or hangings. *Canopy*, with reference to the bed, is the set of hangings that covers and surrounds it. *Tester Bed*, one on which the drapes hang from a tester, which is a sort of flat, quadrangular canopy, the same size as the bed, set above it, near the ceiling of the bedchamber. *Tent Bed*, one in which the hangings have no tester, but the drapes are suspended from a pole, a ring or some other ornament and tied in festoons, or another manner, so that they hang down to enfold the bed, spreading out in the shape of a tent. *Hangings*, all the drapes of a bed, and their accessories, used to conceal it from view, and to defend its occupant from drafts. *Drapery or Curtains*, drapes of the bed, part of the hangings. *Lowered Drapes*, those that have been let down and spread wide to cover the bed. *Raised Drapes*, those that are gathered at the top or sides, on the posts or tied back with cords. *Mosquito Net*, a sort of tent made of netting, or other fine-meshed cloth, that is lowered before entering the bed, to protect its occupant against these extremely tiresome insects at night."

In effect, the canopy bed is the one that comes closest to a contraption, although it is also a classic form. It was to this form that Lenci and Talocci referred in their design I Madrigali 4. "We proposed to Poltrona Frau a design for an apparently traditional bed," recalls Fabio Lenci in an interview he gave to *Casa Oggi* (no. 159, September 1987), "but with a great of technology and electronics hidden inside it… So, instead of starting out from market research, we chose the more courageous course of provocation, with a totally new product, capable of responding to needs that existed at an unconscious level. This bed had a canopy structure of leather-covered steel. From the outside nothing was visible, but on the inside there were a total of thirty-three different functions, all operable from a panel similar to a TV remote control."

In their dictionary of the Italian language, Giacomo Devoto and Giancarlo Oli define the madrigal as a "short literary composition of popular origin, consisting in a vivid picture of pastoral inspiration, often used to convey a gallant tribute." And, in the musical sense, "a musical composition of the *ars antiqua* that reflects the metrical scheme of the poem, initially for two or three voices and then, with the passing of time, increasingly developed in form and in vocal parts, and at times accompanied by the lute." Of the two definitions, perhaps the latter is the most appropriate to Lenci and Talocci's I Madrigali 4, referring to the traditional form of the canopy or four-poster bed as well as to the gradual incorporation of technological functions, taking the contraption further and further toward an exaltation of its playful possibilities and with every part covered with magical, soft and sensual leather. An advanced device, designed to make the most of the time you spend in it, apart from that spent in sleeping and making love. You don't do sums in bed: the figures are lacking. But emotions are multiplied.

"With Luigi Massoni," comments Franco Moschini, "we declared that the sleeping area of the house was a space to be organized to suit the occasion. With Fabio Lenci and Giovanna Talocci we proposed the bed, twenty years later, as a space rendered habitable by technology. I Madrigali 4 also represented a 'test bed' for certain technical developments that we went on to patent and to extend to the whole of our production of upholstered beds: for example the system that allowed the wire mattress to be given a variable profile along the longitudinal axis by means of a rack mechanism. The possibility of altering the elasticity of the sprung surface at several points was fully in keeping with the dictates of the most recent ergonomic research."

The summation of technology was therefore a source of invaluable experience and favored the individual use of the most highly perfected equipment. The presentation of I Madrigali 4 described the bed as follows: "The supporting structure, with four posts and a fitted tester of metal plate, is covered entirely with leather. All the service functions, of which there are over thirty, can be operated with a remote control using infrared light situated between the two backrests. The same control can be used to raise or lower the semitransparent drapes around the bed, making it possible to maintain the space at a different temperature to the rest of the room. A shelf set in the tester can be lowered electronically and used to house a hi-fi system, video recorder, cassette and compact-disc player and projector. The shelf is covered with leather and when not in use vanishes into the tester. The television set is also located here, along with a heating system controlled by a thermostat which gives off heat through unbreakable burnished mirrors. A ventilator serves to circulate air in the area of the bed, scrubbing it with carbon filters to remove smoke and pollution. In addition, there are a humidifier, telephone and small refrigerator set in the back of the bed head, while several displays of adjustable brightness on the bedposts provide information on the temperature, level of humidity, time, alarm setting and selected radio stations, among other things. Two spotlights can be adjusted individually by means of a small joystick in order to provide beams of light for reading."

If in 1987, with I Madrigali 4, Poltrona Frau proposed its own conception of how function and technology could be combined in the home, and ironically emphasized its playful side in a bed that was still a piece of furniture, this was also the year that it came out with a genuine color system applicable to all its stuffed and leather-covered furniture. A fundamental move, aimed at the optimal definition of the types and modes of Frau living.

Models and Modes of Frau Living
From Minuetto to Donald

"What for you is a delightful flower (repository of an idea or source of a feeling) is for me a harmony based on pink lacquer, pale blue, white and pale yellow chilled by a touch of emerald. While never ceasing to be a flower." In 1933, the painter Gianni Maimeri (1884–1951) wrote about his understanding of things in his *Diari*: for him a flower was a harmony of tones, a chromatic blend of different hues when, for others, a flower was simply a flower. So he declared the color to be a structure of the plant, not an aesthetic variant. Matter, and therefore cause, never effect: the flower. Curiously, Paolo Minoli, who was commissioned to develop a color scheme for the leather coverings of Poltrona Frau's upholstered furniture in 1987, also declared the mix of colors to be a structural part of the material. However, the hide removed from the animal to be used as material inevitably changes its natural color into a structural, chromatic artifice in the process of tanning. So while it is the natural harmony of colors that indicates the presence of the flower, artificial color is the mark of Frau leather which, while never ceasing to be leather, is thus able to express the full sense of its refined quality.

From 1987 onward the color of Poltrona Frau upholstered furniture would no longer be a variant of design but a structural definition of the product. "To the indications derived from consumption was added a range of colors more symbolic and representative of the Frau image, including the color known as 'natural leather,'" explained Paolo Minoli in *Casa Oggi* that same year. "We discovered at once that it is a cultural invention rather than a physical fact. The hide is taken from the animal, cut up and tanned: at this point what you ought to get is natural leather, but in reality it is given a bluish tinge by the treatment with chromium salts to which it is subjected. We had to re-create the concept of natural leather 'culturally,' and to do this we decided to examine the colors of all the materials that Poltrona Frau has used in its products by long tradition: down, horsehair, raffia, various types of cotton, etc."

The color, soaking right into the leather, becomes a component of its structure and communicates and sympathizes with the rest of the materials that go to make up the piece of furniture. "Each color we reclaimed became the starting point for a range of colors created by reconstructing all the intermediate shades. From a technical viewpoint, these do not represent gradual, linear transitions, but sinuous curves, in so far as for some lines three colors were revived that did not follow an arithmetic progression in their passage from pale to dark. We shifted each color into paler and darker shades, but also into warmer and colder ones, and we circled around them until we had found the right target, i.e. the color that seemed most pertinent to its use, to the rapport with the leather, with the texture, with the design. It was at once a concrete and a poetic response. This more strictly analytical procedure was followed by one of synthesis: the development of a summarizing scheme that grouped the various 'families' of color according to a scale of brightness, for a total of seventy-three colors. This system allowed for the insertion of new 'families' of color into the broad grid into which they were structured, wherever a gap occurred. This insertion would have to respect the code selected beforehand so that it would be able to establish an organic relationship with the colors already in use. An open-ended system, that could serve as a meta-design for subsequent operations." The system treated color as a component of construction and assigned it the function of a harbinger of the essential equilibrium of the piece of furniture, whose formal definition was made manifest in it. Hence the color was the primary guarantee of the product's authenticity.

However, the system was also a mode of design, when such modes have always been aimed at the equilibrium of the result, an alphabet of understanding, a gauge to measure the truthfulness of the piece of furniture. And so, from 1987 onward, the Color System was added to the stock of know-how that had long been a mark of Poltrona Frau as a company, helping it to give a better configuration to its collection, including the replicas of classic models. Vanity Fair, from 1930, became part of the history of cinema with Bernardo Bertolucci's *The Last Emperor*, released in 1987,

which went on to win a total of nine Oscars: for Best Picture, Direction and Screenplay (to B. Bertolucci, E. Ungari and M. Peploe); for Cinematography (Vittorio Storaro); for Film Editing (Gabriella Cristiani); for Original Score (Ryuichi Sakamoto, David Byrne and Cong Su); for Art Direction (Ferdinando Scarfiotti); for Costume Design (James Acheson); and for Sound (Bill Rowe and Ivan Sharrock). At the age of just three, in 1906, Pu Yi, played by John Lone, was crowned emperor of China. Following the establishment of a republic, in 1912, he was confined to the Forbidden City until his adulthood. When the Japanese invaded Manchuria in the thirties, they permitted him to live a life given over to pleasure. Providing confirmation of the emblematic character of Frau models, Vanity Fair armchairs and couches were used in the scenes from that period. A prisoner in Russia for five years, the last emperor returned to his homeland, where he underwent "reeducation" for ten more and ended his days a "rehabilitated" man, working as a gardener in his former palace, now open to a never-ending flow of tourists.

Thanks in part to the color system that made its products even more meaningful, Poltrona Frau was now capable of manufacturing furniture, whether replicas or new models, that was even more respectful of its surroundings: such as historic buildings, a context that had already been explored at Spoleto in 1984. So when the Teatro Lauro Rossi at Macerata underwent restoration from 1986 to 1989, "for all the associated furnishings," as Giancarlo De Mattia, the architect in charge, declares in the book devoted to his work, "we adhered to the same criteria as were followed in the restoration. Thus we sought to find forms and colors in harmony with the eighteenth-century structure, and ignored the tradition of the nineteenth century, with its red velvets and heavy gold braid. A grosgrain fabric, blue-gray in color, was made specially for the curtains. In the boxes, in addition to salvaging and restoring a type of chair from the time of Samoggia, we decided to adopt the 'Campanino' model of chair, based on the late eighteenth-century tradition and still in production today. For the parquet we used a chair upholstered in leather that had been tanned in a special way, so as to produce a shade of color in perfect harmony with the whole [...] Among the various items of furniture, it proved possible to salvage a number of counters and shelves in a late art nouveau style, which had probably been installed there in the 1920s."

Franco Moschini is particularly proud of the result, which provided official recognition of the design and production of Poltrona Frau, now famous all over the world, in his native region of the Marche. "We took care to match the design as closely as possible," recalls Moschini, "in the restoration as well as in the new furniture. And, on the subject of the former, the chairs for the boxes that De Mattia refers to date back to Luigi Samoggia (1811–1904), a Bolognese decorator who had worked at the theater in Macerata from 1870 to 1871."

In 1986 restoration work started on the Grande Albergo Vesuvio, in Naples. Poltrona Frau took charge of the renovation and furnishing of the hotel's roof-garden, dedicated to Enrico Caruso (1873–1921). "It was necessary to reconcile a number of opposing needs," explains Daniele Baroni, who was in charge of the project along with Keith Gibson, in *Caruso roof-garden*, "such as that of preserving the preexisting typology, as well as taking care to give the setting back its historical image [...]. So it was a question of blending, in a harmonious balance, citations of the past and the advantages of modern comfort, handcrafted objects in tune with the historical tradition and the technical and industrial conception of engineering." The roof-garden is a homage paid, in his native city, to the greatest tenor of all time: Enrico Caruso. Born in Naples, he spent the last days of his life in a suite of

1989: the Berlin Wall collapses.
An East German soldier giving a flower
to young people in Berlin.
On facing page, some graffiti painted
on the Wall.

the Grande Albergo Vesuvio, where he died on August 2, 1921. The main front of the construction, built in the style current during the reign of King Umberto I and inaugurated in 1882, "faces onto the Gulf and offers a view spanning the entire arc of the bay, from Vesuvius to Posillipo Capo and Villa Rosbery at the far end, with the peninsula of Sorrento and the island of Capri in the background." The same gulf that he had sung of and celebrated in theaters all over the world in his full and powerful voice, sweet in timbre and veiled with a touch of melancholy. And so Poltrona Frau, in 1986, took charge of the renovation of the roof-garden in the Neapolitan hotel which, over the course of the twentieth century, has perhaps seen a larger number of illustrious guests

from the worlds of culture and entertainment, as well as heads of state and ruling princes, than any other: the Fumoir replica, armchair and small couch, of the 118 model of 1929, a classic, is now the guarantee of a perfect match between the furnishings and the restored hotel.

Frau replicas are also to be found in that slice of the twentieth century which came out in 1987 under the title *La famiglia* (*The Family*) and was directed by Ettore Scola. The movie chronicles eighty years in the life of the family, from 1906 to 1986, and is located entirely in a middle-class apartment in Rome, where the minimal signs of daily existence reflect the events taking place outside. The furniture changes style as the generations succeed one another, apart from a

few significant heirlooms: the 1919, a replica of the 128 of 1919, is the armchair used by Carlo, played by Vittorio Gassman. Its presence testifies to the continuity of the family right to the end, in the study where Carlo, now a retired professor of literature, sits and explains the verses of Giosuè Carducci's *San Martino* to his little grandson.

Certainly the form of the armchair, in its most classical sense of a soft and comfortable refuge, is an unmistakable presence symbolizing the continuity of affections that link it indissolubly to its family of origin, to the person who best represents it or did so in the past. This is the case with the fine evocation of Pietro in *Con gli occhi chiusi* by Federigo Tozzi (1883–1920). "He thought of the lamp, so still and always the same, with its tin bell. He thought of mom's armchair, which had a sort of wooden drawer underneath the cushion in which she had kept her balls of wool and the only two books she possessed, illustrated novels published in installments. He thought of the four cushions on which she used to recline; each of them was

Minuetto, 1989, designed by Gae Aulenti. An elegant couch seating two people and designed to encourage conversation. On facing page, Minuetto and the pyramid of the Musée du Louvre in Paris, designed by I.M. Pei, 1989.

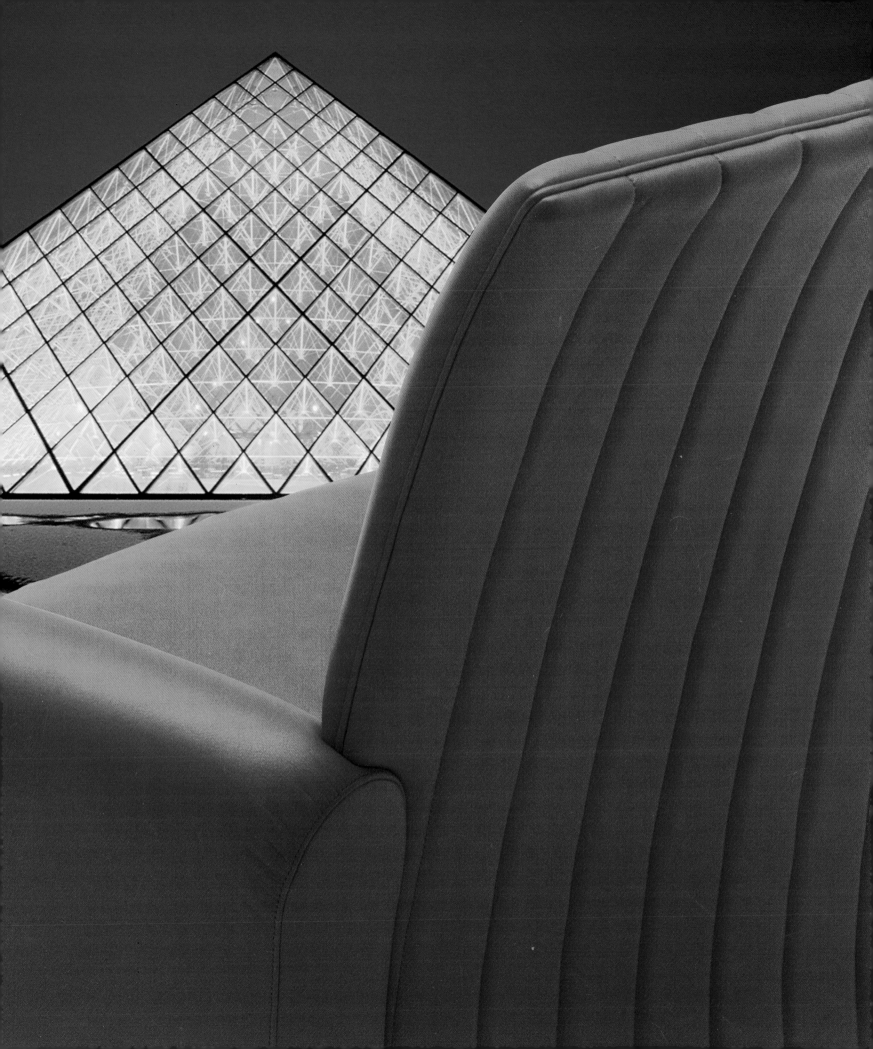

Intervista, 1989, designed by Lella and Massimo Vignelli. The chair, conceived for the TG2 studio of Rai, the Italian state television company, was intended to meet the particular needs of the newscast to which its name, Interview, refers. One of the modes of Frau living in its most public appearance: television.

deformed in a recognizable way. He thought of the scent of eau-de-cologne, of the bottles of antihysteric, of a worn golden crucifix."

It was to the significance of the chair in the home that Poltrona Frau again turned its attention in 1989, this time transforming it, with Gae Aulenti's Minuetto, into a place for conversation: an elegant couch seating two people and designed to encourage talk. A popular dance in the seventeenth century, the minuet is a figuration of sociality. It so fascinated King Louis XIV of France that he made it a court ritual. And the placing of two or more pieces of furniture opposite one another was even closer to the musical figuration, so that Minuetto seemed to become a participant in the dance it was named after. Thus it met the need for intimacy at a time when, outside the home, in the city, squares, gardens and park benches in particular had ceased to be places favorable to socializing. Minuetto revived the distinctly popular sense of a place for conversation, but in the privacy of the home. And this was part of the "experimentalism" to which Angelo Cortesi referred in *Letteratura & scienza*, defining it as a "current": "The term itself renders its definition difficult. Rather than by its products, it can be distinguished by its attitude and approach to design. Each product represents a line of research and presupposes a result that is always different, even from the viewpoint of form [as well as] a direct relationship with scientific and social aspects,

attributing to them a comprehensible language. Under some circumstances the process by which a product is created or a piece of research carried out is revealed through the design. Many exponents of this current are working to introduce the culture of design into services in the public sphere, with a view to improving their formal qualities and efficiency [...]. Its exponents are: G. Aulenti, A. Mangiarotti, Castelli Design Milano (Clino Castelli), Studio D.A., Studio MID, A. Cortesi, King and Miranda. Gae Aulenti declares: 'Any object made by human beings, be it a monument or a refuge, cannot escape its relationship with the city, the place of representation of the human condition. So its analysis is only possible if the object can be defined as a discontinuous form of the whole: if the way in which it finds its place and the rules determining its appearance can be demonstrated. The existence of the object is conceived in the positive terms of its relationship with the city.'"

The presentation of Minuetto stresses the choice of the most comprehensible language. "Around the middle of the last century, armchairs and couches became increasingly stuffed,

sometimes to the point of absurdity, and only in a few cases, such as the Chesterfields, did they constitute a precise structural vocabulary that was quickly translated into tradition. Even in recent times there has been an alternative between opulent forms of upholstery and others with a more elegant and essential design. Gae Aulenti has chosen the second course, creating a couch for two people (which favors socializing and conversation more than other types of furniture) based on modern habits of sitting and in line with an up-to-date conception of ergonomics. A light, airy and dynamic structure that allows the body to assume comfortable positions. By contrast, the leather and upholstery, finished by hand, is inspired by the classical canons for which Poltrona Frau is renowned and places the emphasis on softness and pliability. The covering of the couch, in high-quality calfskin and the Frau range of colors, underlines the extreme grace of its function." Thus Minuetto rehabilitated the piece of upholstered furniture as a place of conversation. However, in Lella and Massimo Vignelli's design of a coordinated image for the Tg2 television studio of the RAI, in that same year of 1989, the seating was provided by Intervista: a chair named after the particular type of broadcast for which the studio was used, the interview. In this case the design was intended to make it easier for television cameras to frame the sitter from various points of the studio as he or she was subjected to the crossfire of questions. It also permitted the guest to assume the correct position of the diaphragm so as to improve the carrying power of his or her voice. Thus it was the product of a targeted ergonomic design. Even though, as the presentation clearly explained, this aim did not invalidate the Frau identity: "Apart from the specific use for which it was created, Intervista is conceptually a Frau armchair, in the uniqueness of its form, the elegance of its design and the manual skill involved in its construction." So from 1989 onward, one of the Frau modes of living was present in the Tg2 studio, in its most public manifestation: on television. However the armchair did not remain confined to this role, but entered into private life as well, in the derived form of a two-seater couch, which revealed its potential as a proper piece of furniture. Leather couches and armchairs have always been islands of refined, sensual intimacy, be they of moderate or ample dimensions: comfortable wombs, as Fulvio Tomizza describes them in *L'amicizia*. "I was attracted above all by his warm nest: the soft drawing room with ample couches upholstered in leather that was almost white, tall armchairs, even the fireplace, undoubtedly a well-stocked bar, drapes with which to attenuate the light by day while by night illumination would be provided by various crystal

Frau Car. Original Pininfarina drawing of the interior of the Ferrari Mythos, 1989.

Sketch of the Ferrari Mythos, 1989. The Mythos at Spoleto in 1990. Paolo Pininfarina comments: "In 1990 we... put the Mythos prototype... on show at Spoleto... It turned out not to be so easy though: the Mythos... wouldn't go through an ancient doorway. We were obliged to construct a sort of 'Leonardesque' machine that allowed us to turn the car on its side and take it into the exhibition space that way."

chandeliers, floor lamps, the candelabrum on the piano, perhaps even the light from an adjoining room."

In 1989, Frau upholstered furniture served to seat guests and broadcasters on a variety of television programs: Vanity Fair was used by Emilio on Odeon TV, Cartolina by Andrea Barbato and Interlude on *Mai Dire Mai*. In its efforts to get its models into the studios, Poltrona Frau was continuing the policy pursued by Renzo in his time, when the technology of the image was limited to the silent film. If located in the president's study, the boardroom or the other haunts of top management, however, leather couches and armchairs were capable of assuming all the seriousness of their role, while maintaining intact their qualities of softness and comfort. "Our color system," explains Franco Moschini, "allows them to fit into the most classic architectural setting as well as the most decidedly innovative one. There was on our part a willingness to explore further the management setting we had already entered with the Antropovarius range. We were equally interested in reestablishing links with the world of automobile design, as a mark of continuity with the history of Frau."

And what better opportunity could arise than a renewal of the collaboration with Pininfarina? "Franco Moschini," comments Paolo Pininfarina, "reminded me that Renzo Frau had known my grandfather Pinin, back in the days when he was working with his brother Giovanni, and had collaborated on the upholstery of some of his exclusive models. He was very interested in picking up the thread of the relationship that the founders of our respective companies had formed in the

twenties. The occasion presented itself in 1989, when we decided to have Poltrona Frau upholster the interior of the Mythos." A truly exceptional occasion, as Mythos was a milestone. "In 1989, twenty-four years after the presentation of the Dino Berlinetta Speciale one-design research prototype in 1965," I noted in *Pininfarina. Identity of a Design*, "Pininfarina produced the Ferrari Mythos. Five years had passed since the debut of the Testarossa series and Mythos used the same, proven mechanics. 'A car of great technical and formal accomplishments,' declares Sergio, 'the Mythos consists of two vehicles, one inside the other. The one at the back, stronger and bigger, carries the engine, the one at the

The Meeting Chair Ego, 1990,
designed by Pininfarina Extra.
Top models of the nineties.

front cleaves, penetrates and is streamlined.' Augusto Morello has examined the topological characteristics of the formal treatment: 'With its two tori, triangular in plan and inserted one inside the other, it recalls the disturbing topology of the Klein bottle. It is a textbook example of how to define a *Gestalt*, a configuration that should be seen as *form*, i.e. connected with the world and not just with the vehicle, rather than as *shape*, i.e. mere aesthetic stimulus. In this sense Mythos, a Ferrari, is an interpretation that would have seemed a completely new phenotype of automobile even to Pinin and Ferrari, champions of realistic utopianism.' The Mythos, notwithstanding the highly innovative character of its technical and aesthetic solutions, remained an automobile and for this very reason was the Ferrari that Pinin Farina and Drake would have wanted. But the Mythos went well beyond the Testarossa, and in this sense was even more of a Ferrari than the most celebrated Ferrari of the moment. As Lorenzo Ramaciotti points out: 'The mechanics of the Ferrari Testarossa are an ideal starting point for formal research of this kind: the exceptional performance, the structure with the engine in the middle and the radiator at the side, the charisma of the Prancing Horse: all these represent a spur and a stimulus to be daring... In the development of the project technical and functional qualities have not been sacrificed in the quest for a strong formal presence. Two mobile aerodynamic appendages, a lip at the front and a wing at the back, move into position on the attainment of a preestablished speed. The body is constructed out of composite material and is completely removable, in the manner of competition vehicles. In movement, on the road, the car is a demonstration of balance between aesthetic values and technical rationality.'" And here Paolo Pininfarina recalls an amusing episode: "In 1990 we were happy to put the Mythos prototype, which had already produced a very positive reaction all over the world over the course of 1989, on show at Spoleto, at that year's Festival of Two Worlds, alongside another legendary car of ours, the Cisitalia of 1947. It turned out not to be so easy though: the Mythos, we realized when we got there, wouldn't go through an ancient doorway. We were obliged to construct a sort of 'Leonardesque' machine that allowed us to turn the car on its side and take it into the exhibition space that way."

Mythos was to open the road to Maranello for Poltrona Frau, establishing the contacts that would later lead to the prestigious contract for the leather upholstery of Ferrari production models intended for the most exclusive of customers all over the world. "With the Antropovarius Office range," explains Franco Moschini, "we had extended the sense of Frau living to the world of management, but we knew we

The President model in the Ego range; the Meeting Chair, of moderate dimensions but extremely comfortable, performs the function for which it is designed. In the background, illuminated offices in the skyscrapers of Los Angeles.

were ready to go further in this direction, with the aim of underlining further the exclusive nature of our furniture. For this reason we commissioned the design of a new series from Pininfarina: we had always been amazed by the studio's magical, indisputable capacity to innovate without ever giving in to the lures of current fashion."

This was in 1990, the year of Ego. "The series with this name," explains Paolo Pininfarina, "comprised the President, Executive and Meeting Chair models. A table with a base hollowed out of solid marble, cylindrical in shape, and a beechwood top covered entirely with leather and with an elliptical inlay of marble completed the series, along with a console table made from the same materials. We wanted to make the prestige of Ego evident through the use of noble materials: marble and leather. A research prototype to all intents and purposes, the table could still be adapted for production, even if only in limited numbers. The same was true of the President armchair, conceived as a genuine operations center, equipped with a remote control that would allow its occupant to operate all the electronic systems located in the room in which it was placed.

Drawing by Luca Scacchetti for the Hydra series, 1992, from the album *La collezione Hydra*. On facing page, a detail of Guercino's *Study for Hercules Killing the Hydra*, 1618, private collection.

with expanded-polyurethane padding, while the seat was sprung with elastic straps. The four castors attached to the frame allowed the upholstered chair to be moved around. Thus the Ego range fell within the program of upgrading the workplace that Poltrona Frau intended to pursue.

"Having reached the peak of a rapid and unpredictable process of evolution in the field of working activities linked to the tertiary sector, the question arises of whether concentration of the workforce in a large building should still be considered a frame of reference for the modern business. There are now a number of other, fairly well-established trends, from buildings of architectural prestige but more modest dimensions to the conversion of historic buildings, in which there is a tendency to humanize imposing spaces with elegant and comfortable furnishings." This was the direction taken by Poltrona Frau in 1990, when Franco Moschini took total control of the company. By this time thirty years had passed since his decision to take it under his wing and the delicate operation, carried out through the Milan branch of the Bankers Trust Company of New York, was a fitting reward for his determination both to maintain continuity and to develop the project he had undertaken. Poltrona Frau was by now a recognized force. "In constant, continuous expansion on international markets, its deep roots in Italy, often founded on relationships of collaboration that have lasted for decades, act as a counter-

However, it proved impossible to do this, as the cabling in the seat could not yet be standardized. So Ego President was brought into production in a simplified version, thanks to its lines fully in keeping with Frau classicism, along with the Executive. Of the three Egos, however, Meeting Chair is undoubtedly the best known and most widely used in management settings. The modest-sized but extremely comfortable chair performs the task for which it was designed."

According to the presentation of Ego President, Executive and Meeting Chair: "The steel structure is combined with padding made of expanded polyurethane shaped in molds. A quilt of cotton wadding is located immediately under the leather covering. The base is set on rotating, self-blocking, soft castors." The Meeting Chair also had a steel structure

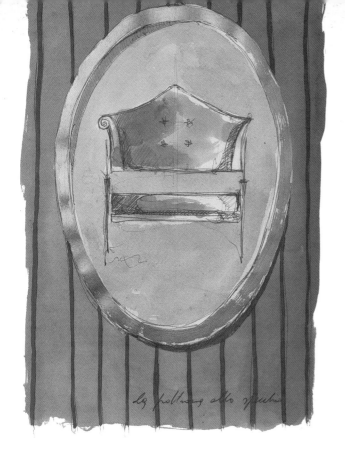

balance to ramifications that extend right through Europe, as well as America and the Far East."

Since 1998 Frau Avio has availed itself of the external consultancy of Tito Agnoli, who in 1989 had designed the interiors of the A109 Agusta, where "the solutions are in the realm of ergonomic and perceptual comfort: study of the padding, and therefore of kidney supports, the inclination of the seat and the choice of color for the leather used to upholster the seats and paneling, as well as the whole range of accessories." Frau Car, Frau Contract and Frau Residencial are establishing themselves as divisions sensitive to the needs of a potential market that is increasingly demanding.

The Research and Development Center handles the connection between design, craftsmanship and technology, through the Technical Department, Testing Workshop and Prototype Workshop, all of which use CAD to ensure that the company maintains perfect control over its progressive and continuous evolution. The registered office of Poltrona Frau is still in Turin, while the management, administration and production facilities are housed in a building of seventeen thousand square meters on a site with an area of a hundred and twenty-nine thousand. The common denominator of the company's extremely varied interests remains the intention to render the concept of Frau living as broad as possible.

So it was that in 1992, Poltrona Frau found itself once again on the Olympian heights of the world of cinema. In fact in one of the most internationally popular American movies of recent times, Mick Jackson's *The Bodyguard*, starring Kevin Costner, Whitney Houston, Gary Kemps, Bill Cobbs and Tomas Arana: the scene is set in the home of the rock star Rachel Marron, played by Whitney Houston, and the huge sitting room on the ground floor is unmistakably furnished with the Vanity Fair replica of the 900. Unlike in Bernardo Bertolucci's *Last Emperor* of 1987, however, where the furniture was a precise historical reference to the date, 1930, here it is a timeless model, capable of fitting in with any décor. And this is just how the Vanity Fair armchairs and couches appear, even in the make-believe world of the cinema, when in the opening sequences of the movie, Frank Farmer, the bodyguard played by Kevin Costner, turns up at the singer's home, determined to carry out the job for which he has been hired to the best of his ability.

Outside the movies, however, Poltrona Frau took a new and above all innovative step in its efforts to pursue excellence in furnishing, bringing out a model in 1992 that bore a name redolent with all the fantasy of classical mythology: Hydra, monstrous serpent with many heads, capable of sprouting new ones when they were cut off by the hero. "Moschini asked me to come up with a modern piece, but one that

Drawings by Luca Scacchetti for Hydra and an armchair from the Hydra series, 1992.

Irony is a distinctive feature of Hydra,
for Luca Scacchetti shows that he was
capable of turning the furnishing
of the house into a game, seeking
the complicity of its potential tenant,
while Hydra guarantees the place,
the way of Frau living.

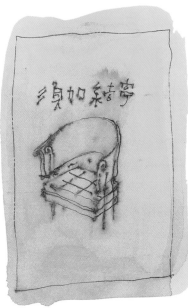

would be absolutely Frau. I accepted willingly," recalls Luca Scacchetti, "and showed him, after about twenty days, a sort of picture diary, a collection of drawings. This was Hydra, or rather the graphic statement of its conceptual formulation. A seat in checked leather, essentially that of the Le Corbusier and Mies van der Rohe models, standing on metal legs typical of rationalism, although reworked so that they resembled the samurai swords I had admired on my recent trip to Japan. A zone above this and detached from it, the back, assumed a variety of different shapes, growing increasingly baroque. Now that we have been freed forever from period or reproduction chairs, and sit on strictly up-to-date structures, we can at last permit ourselves to indulge in decoration, allowing the shape of the back to represent a journey through the different ages of upholstered furniture.

Moschini was very taken with this interpretation of mine and decided to put Hydra into production, though he placed limits on the range of backs." In the preface to Luca Scacchetti's picture diary *La collezione Hydra*, Daniele Baroni writes: "It cannot be considered just an ordinary design commissioned by a manufacturer specializing in the sector. The well-known background and image of

Frau fits in perfectly with Scacchetti's idea of retracing the history of the couch and armchair, including that predating the company's foundation. As is well-known, in fact, the most significant types of upholstered furniture were developed in the eighteenth century, shortly before the beginning of the Industrial Revolution. Yet this is just a coincidence, since the production of these objects has always been a craft activity. The whole upholstery trade, even more than that of cabinetmaking, has always escaped the processes of high industrialization and mass production. What has changed over time is the style. First this type of furniture, like others, had to adapt to the stylistic dictates of the courts of kings and emperors. Then it came under the influence of the anonymous tradition of Middle Eastern exoticism, or that of the Anglo-Saxon bourgeoisie, emerging out of Victorian society, which gained a grip on the whole of the modern

world. The program devised by Luca Scacchetti entailed a lexical articulation, in which the architect syntactically removed the components of the exclusively functional structure at the core of the upholstered chair, i.e. the seat as support for the body, leaving the back with freedom of expression and the role of semantic interpretation." The chair was presented as follows: "The structure of the seats is made out of aluminum profile. A soft layer of pre-compressed Dacron is set on top of the expanded polyurethane stuffing. The structure of the back is made out of padded curved wood. The vertical supports linking the seat and back are in chromed metal, as is the central insert, with a cup of blown glass or turned marble..." And Baroni again, talking about the designer: "He introduced a new element,

The Hydra armchair, a permanent guest on the Rai Uno television program *Porta a Porta*. On facing page, two images of Hydra showing the extreme flexibility of the series.

never envisaged hitherto; interchangeability of style, something which went far beyond the modest functional concept of removable cushion covers. It is clear from the design that Scacchetti had no intention of radically altering this type of furniture. Rather, drawing on what had been consolidated over time and taking a playful and gently ironic approach, he limited himself to composing and combining its elements, giving the chair a different connotation each time." Irony is a distinctive feature of Hydra, for Luca Scacchetti showed that he was capable of turning the furnishing of the house into a game, seeking the complicity of its potential tenant, while Hydra guaranteed the place, the way of Frau living. On the other hand Poltrona Frau considers every aspect of its production a question of design, from furniture intended for the home to that made to fulfill a particular contract. In fact work orders for both types are not given a

The woman's world of the nineties:
Susan Sarandon and Geena Davis
in *Thelma and Louise*; a Prada model
of the 1999–2000 fall-winter collection;
the Spice Girls, icons of British pop.
Lara Croft, heroine of the Play Station
video game *Tomb Raider*; the Trussardi
boutique at Palazzo Marino alla Scala
in Milan, renovated to a design
by Pierluigi Cerri, opened in 1996.

progressive number or code, but bear the name of whoever has commissioned the furniture. The game still entails responsibility: to the product and to the client, both understood in a physical sense.

"When we were offered the chance to make an armchair with Richard Meier for the Getty Center," writes Franco Moschini in the preface to the fine book of photographs by Antonia Mulas devoted to the American architect's work, "I was immediately aware of the responsibility and the commitment that we would have to take on. Then came the daily work of our technicians, the precise responses to the designer's requirements, enriched each time by enthusiasm and by mutual pleasure in the work... These convictions and this experience reassured me about the positive outcome of our labors, but it was when the work was over, looking at that armchair created in the setting of one of the most superb examples of contemporary architecture, that I felt certain

A view of Hollywood Boulevard,
Los Angeles, California; the Getty
Center in Los Angeles, California,
designed by Richard Meier.
On facing page, West Coast armchair,
designed by Richard Meier, 1996,
for the Getty Center in Los Angeles.

once again about the true 'mission' of Poltrona Frau: measuring ourselves against the best designers in the world and bringing to the collaboration our flexibility, our specific skills and our artisan spirit applied to an industrial context. A commitment that we bring to everything we do and that is part of the genetic inheritance of the whole company."

So in 1996, twelve years after the restoration of the former church of San Gregoriuccio alla Sinagoga in Spoleto, which had marked the debut of Frau Contract with the fitting out of the Sala Frau as a new venue for the Festival of Two Worlds, and seven after the furnishing of the Teatro Lauro Rossi in Macerata, bringing recognition to Poltrona Frau in its own region of the Marche as well, the company took its experience with design and production over the ocean, to

are able to wander around. The small flights of steps that lead to the museum are also part of that space. It is a whole progression of public spaces, precisely because it is public. So many people come to visit the Getty Center: they interact with each other as well as with the art." Antonia Mulas writes: "The ideal Renaissance city has been reinvented by Richard Meier, an architect who knows Italy well and loves the country. The round temple, at Brentwood, is modern, gigantic, white. Around it a science-fiction city is growing up, a series of buildings constructed out of various materials, magnificent, lavish and perfect. An astounding and yet harmonious phenomenon, with its mix of the medieval, the Renaissance, the Wailing Wall and a transatlantic liner with gleaming handrails, floating on a sea of urban areas scat-

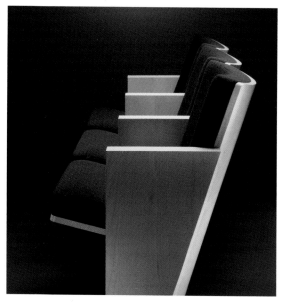

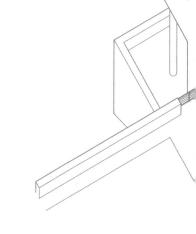

West Coast armchair, 1996.
Axonometric cutaway of the auditorium of the Getty Center in Los Angeles.

apply them in the context of one of the century's most sensational works of architecture. A. Mulas: "You have created a well-defined architectural complex in an area as vast as Los Angeles, which lacks a single center." R. Meier: "I looked for a modern way to express the centrality of the Renaissance. With a complex institution like the Getty Center it is necessary to give the spaces a hierarchy, a certain order. In the Getty center I created several centers, not just one. The first central location on the outside is the plaza, the area where visitors arrive when they get off the streetcar at the top of the hill. The plaza is a public space, just like the one at the heart of a city. People get off the streetcar and see other people, some of them seated, others drinking coffee. It is a decompression zone, a meeting place, where people

tered without any order or centrality: Los Angeles… What could I do in a situation so much bigger than me? I told myself, photograph whatever you can as the instinct takes you, and that's what I did. This led me to stroll around and quickly snap the elements that attracted me, that light that was always changing and completely altering what I had seen a few hours earlier. A constant movement of volumes in the sunlight, strong shadows on the ground and winding like spirals around the white columns of enameled steel, modern trellises of grapes and flowers like the ones I remembered against the pale blue background of the cloister of Santa Chiara in Naples. Clouds reflected in the glass, white, metaphysical staircases leading up to the sky, in an obsessive repetition that became a language." And going

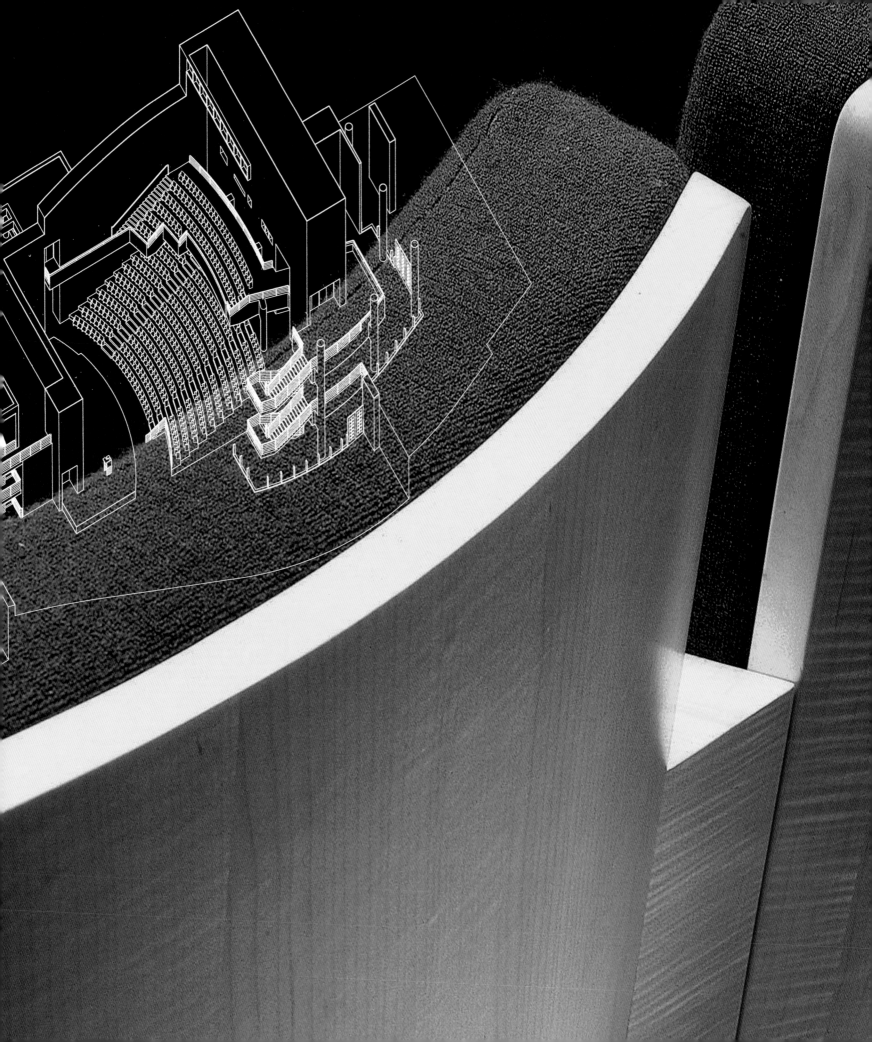

A view of the interior of the European Parliament in Strasbourg and the Monsieur Paul armchair, designed by Avant Travaux Architecture, 1996.

having created such an extraordinary place." A. Mulas: "I was commissioned to take these photographs of the Getty Center by Poltrona Frau. How did you find working with this Italian company?" R. Meier: "We wanted to design special chairs for the auditorium, something that would match the quality of the rest of the Getty Center. This firm was ready to work with us, to produce what we designed. Not all manufacturers are prepared to undertake something like that. And then Frau's production was already of high quality, so we were certain that they would create a good product." A curious remark this, they were "ready to work with us, to produce what we designed." On first sight, in fact, the statement seems totally obvious, given that it is the designer's task to give the object its shape and the manufacturer's to make it. Yet Meier goes on to reveal the true nature of the accord: understanding and respect for the design, the same respect that, in turn, he shows for Poltrona Frau. "Working with the best designers," comments Giampiero Pistacchi, "brings us great satisfaction and teaches us a lot. It is also a way to gauge our ability to interpret their different requirements. That's how it was with Marco Zanuso, when we made the chair for the Piccolo Teatro: while the prototype confirmed the great designer's precision, the details of the mechanisms that affected the dynamics of the object also confirmed our determination to demonstrate its feasibility. It is in this spirit that we accept the challenge each time and set out to meet the client's expectations: this was as true in the case of a highly rigorous chair like Richard Meier's West Coast for the auditorium of the Getty Center, made entirely of wood and with an upholstered seat and back, which we are now using for other supply contracts, as it was in that of Avant Travaux's Monsieur Paul, in 1996, the new seat for the European Parliament in Strasbourg: an imposing armchair, equipped with a mechanism for shifting it forward and backward and arms that could be raised to allow the sitter more freedom of movement. Described as a 'throne for the third millennium,' the project was concluded in

back to the conversation between architect and photographer. A. Mulas: "How do you feel after coming to the end of such an extraordinary and complex experience, an experience to which you devoted fourteen years of your life? Do you feel a sense of emptiness?" R. Meier: "At the beginning it was very hard. There was a period of down when we'd finished. It had been very absorbing going back and forth every month for so many years. At first I asked myself, and now what do I do? But then new opportunities arose, new challenges. The predominant feeling was one of pride in

Details of the Monsieur Paul armchair created especially for the hemicycle of the European Parliament in Strasbourg.

1999 and represents the most demanding contract we have fulfilled up to now."

In a press release issued in France on October 9, 1996, Poltrona Frau declared: "Through our subsidiary Frau France, Poltrona Frau's contract division has won the international competition for the supply of all the furnishings for the hemicycle of the new building of the European Parliament in Strasbourg. This is undoubtedly a commission of great prestige that does honor first of all to the Italian furniture industry and assigns particular significance to the design and production methods of the Italian school. All this is founded on the constant quality of the upholstered furniture for domestic use that Poltrona Frau has been producing since 1912"; in other

words, on the quality of the approach to design inaugurated by Renzo Frau at the beginning of the twentieth century, maintained by Savina Pisati in the thirties and renewed and perfected by Franco Moschini, who assumed the mantle in 1962. "The new complex of the European Parliament, which constitutes an authentic scheme of urban development, was designed by Architecture Studio Europe of Paris. For the design team, the work of architecture aspired to the status of a symbol, a strong signal conveying a certain idea of Europe that is filled with meaning. An architecture that could reflect the ties that bind the community together and present a significant image of its Parliament. A global image, or rather a corporate identity, summing up a pregnancy and a unifying force, with the aim of overcoming all lin-

Dario Fo receiving the Nobel Prize for Literature from King Carl XVI Gustaf of Sweden in 1997.
On facing page, Lola chair, designed by Pierluigi Cerri, 1997.

guistic barriers. Just as Europe itself is considered a work-in-progress, i.e. a mission not yet accomplished, its cylindrical architecture is intended to evoke a geometric form that rises upward, only to stop at an 'unfinished' stage. A reference to the mythical Tower of Babel or an invitation to the architects of the future to finish the job? Among the many citations that can be discerned in this description, there are undoubtedly references to those masters of utopian architecture, Boullée and Ledoux. The large hemicycle used for meetings of the parliamentarians, along with numerous other meeting rooms on the upper levels and along the perimeter, was to be the setting for the furnishings designed by Avant Travaux Architectures for Architecture Studio

Europe. Poltrona Frau would construct over five thousand seats and four thousand five hundred desks for the members of parliament and for use in the meeting rooms and translation booths, as well as other pieces of furniture."

With reference to the Hydras used on *Porta a Porta*, the Intervista on Tg2 and the Monsieur Paul in the Parliament at Strasbourg, Enzo Biagi appears to have exclaimed: "It's not the politicians we should blame if they don't get up anymore, but Poltrona Frau for making their chairs too comfortable."

A quip that Renzo would probably have liked: he might even have talked to Golia about using it in one of his posters. "The experience gained in the various Contract and

"Its construction relied on the manual skills of our master automobile upholsterers, who molded the leather onto a structure made of polyurethane with a metal insert."

Car divisions," concludes Giampiero Pistacchi, "has been useful to our proposals in the field of domestic furniture. The special method we developed to handle the leather covering of dashboards in cars found further application in the Lola of 1997, a refined design by Pierluigi Cerri. Its construction relied on the manual skills of our master automobile upholsterers, who molded the leather onto a structure made of polyurethane with a metal insert." It was only in appearance that the Lola chair contrasted with the nature of its components. While it was indeed sophisticated technologies that made it possible to use polyurethanes in the most appropriate way, the leather and its color were equally the result of targeted technological research.

In his essay "L'arte e la tecnologia moderna," Carlo Giulio Argan wrote: "It is worth pointing out that industry was not, in itself, a new cycle that commenced when the artisan one came to an end. Craft and industry have coexisted since remote times and the distinction between them corresponds, roughly speaking, to the one between the production of individual objects and mass production. Nor are the categories completely separate. It was not unusual for the two processes, those of craft and industry, to overlap and intertwine: often industry had limited itself to broadening the range of consumers for models produced by craftsmen and at other times craftsmen had turned to industry for some initial phases in the working of raw materials. But industrial production had always remained subordinate: as it was being asked to repeat, it could not be asked to invent as well, except perhaps its own tools. The so-called industrial revolution did not consist so much in the introduction of new sources of power, new tools and new ways of organizing labor, as in a reversal of the scale of values. There can be no doubt that industry today produces many things that could not be produced by artisans and that (except in the cases where they have survived on the basis of their rarity value) handicrafts are located at an inferior level to the articles produced by industry. What does this turn-around signify? The crafts, at the peak of their splendor, placed the highest value on the unique and unrepeatable piece (the work of art); i.e. the maximum quality was identified with the minimum quantity: the one-off piece had an infinite value, the piece produced in an infinite series a limited value. Industry, on the other hand, places the highest value on the series: the article can be produced in thousands without losing anything of its quality; on the contrary, is value lies precisely in the fact that it is repeated and repeatable. It is clear that this change in values in the world of manufacturing corresponds to a change in values in society: value has shifted from the individual to the series of individuals, and therefore from society as a system of differentiated individual activities to the mass, where the individual is subsumed in the category."

Precisely because of its artisan character, Poltrona Frau does not fall within the framework of this last analysis. It sees its way of tackling design as craft, and design as the essence of its craft. A way that, in fact, leads it to experiment with the most advanced techniques and to exploit them by choice whenever it is opportune to do so, out of the necessities of the particular occasion. Then the fact that it sees its own craft methods as design leads it to an awareness of the value of its own stock of know-how, and to its continual enrichment, something that allows it to go on evolving without ever losing its identity. And finally, it is precisely the choice based on necessity, linked to the particular project, that always brings Frau's mode of operation back to the human being. If the company's philosophy also embraces the mass production of furniture, this does not result in the transformation of individual consumers into a mass, as the user is still making a choice, a choice that by definition is one of quality.

The user chooses his or her own way of living, which is even true on the level of the community. This was confirmed, again in 1997, by Ferdinand Alexander Porsche's Nuwelle, a small armchair intended for conference halls. From an ergonomic viewpoint, the object draws on the study carried out for the Antropovarius range and solves the problems posed by limited space, which makes it necessary to place the rows close together and causes inconvenience to anyone who has to make their way between them. Nuwelle has a depth of only twenty-eight centimeters, considerably improving conditions in small halls and increasing the capacity of larger ones. As the presentation declares: "The system is based on a cylindrical metal structure which functions as a beam, attached to the floor by a pillar that terminates in a pedestal. The body of the seat and back, as well as the structure, is made out of self-supporting composite material, produced in a mold and painted. The padding is made of fireproof and non-deformable polyurethane. The seat folds down automatically by means of a mechanical pivoting system. And the arm moves into place simultaneously. A suitable mechanism ensures that it returns to the stand-up position solely when the seat is raised. The writing surface, set inside the arm, is partially retractable and easy to pull out." Thus the configuration is one of a form dynamic in its function and use that

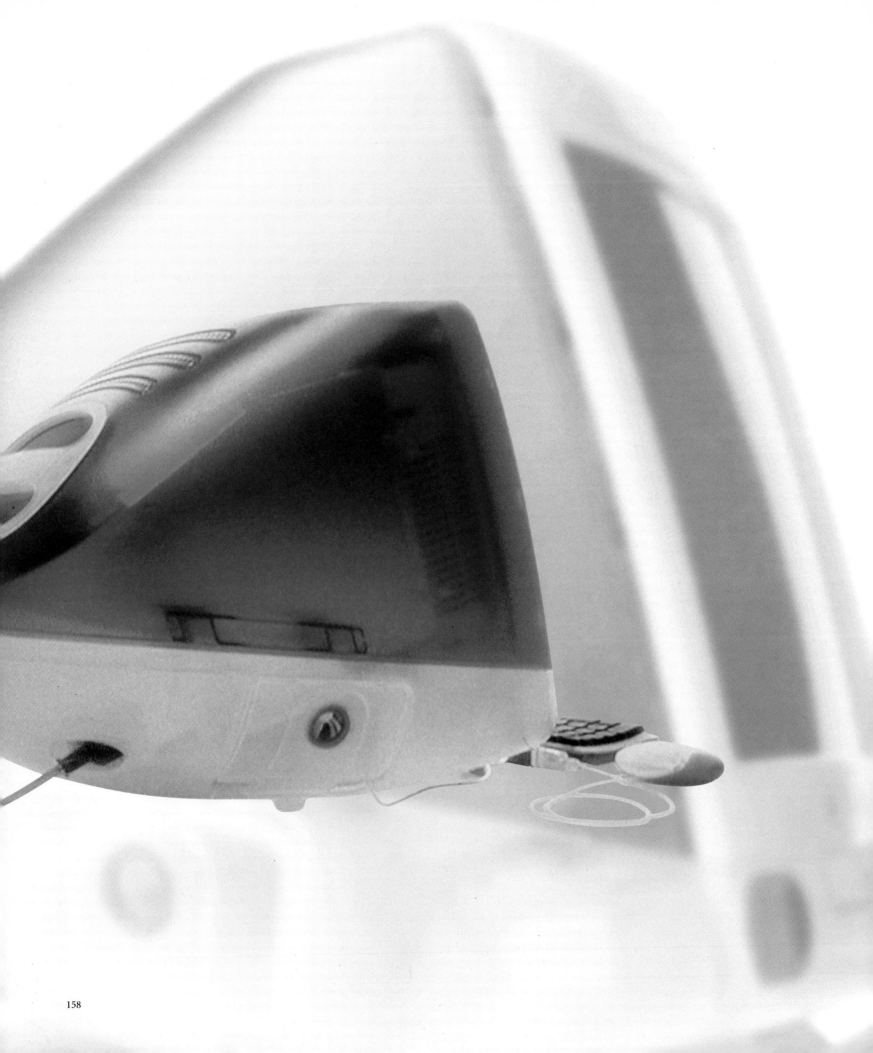

takes up the minimum of space when the seat is not in use. The ergonomic study was concerned not only with making the chair comfortable, but also with the way it folded: in comparison with other models present on the market, in fact, the seat leaves more room between the rows.

Pierluigi Cerri's Lola and Ferdinand Alexander Porsche's Nuwelle were both brought out in 1997, as objects for use in different settings. What they had in common, however, was the sense of Frau living. The same sense that Poltrona Frau's Car division extended and perfected in 1998, concluding the negotiations with Maranello begun ten years earlier, at the time when it did the upholstery of the Pininfarina research possible to shift all that horsepower in front: the Ferrari 456 GT was born. 'I was struck,' recalls Sergio, 'by the views of certain critics, ready to make hasty judgments: Pininfarina, after all, had simply redesigned the Daytona. If after all of twenty-four years, up until the birth of the 456, the Daytona had still not been forgotten, then this was something to boast rather than get upset about. All the more so since we were well aware that we had surpassed it, without forgetting its compactness, its grit and the extreme elegance of its lines.' At the Palazzo dell'Arte of the Milan Triennale, in 1993, a panel of judges made up of distinguished personalities from the worlds of culture, art and architecture awarded the 456 GT

  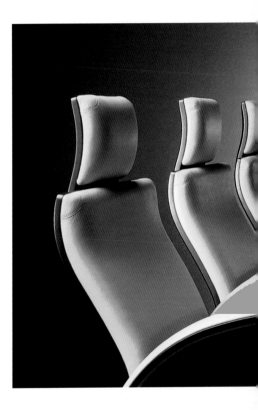

prototype Mythos and received the commission for the leather upholstery of the interiors of the 456 GT, which went into production in 1992. "In 1968, the Daytona," I noted in *Pininfarina. Identity of a Design,* "marked the limit of reliability for a high-performance car, with the engine at the front, and in 1984, the Testarossa enhanced the reliability of a centrally-positioned motor. In 1992 advances in the technology for control of the vehicle made it possible to opt, according to the needs of the design, for either of the two solutions, both of them safe. The central engine, however, barely left room for two seats. So when it came to designing a Gran Turismo sports car, with four seats, it at last proved

Nuwelle, 1997, designed by Ferdinand Alexander Porsche. From an ergonomic viewpoint, Nuwelle, intended for conference halls, draws on the study carried out for the Antropovarius range.
On facing page, the I-Mac computer, a typical example of late-nineties design.

Some Ferrari interiors upholstered
by Poltrona Frau:
the Ferrari 360 Modena of 1999,
the 550 Maranello of 1996
and the 456 GT of 1992.

the prize for the most beautiful automobile in the world. They declared its form to be a contribution to the figurative culture of our time. A similar recognition had been given to the Cisitalia, at the MoMA, some fifty years earlier. Looking at the vehicle from the outside, what catches your eye are the curved surfaces marked by lines of tension and hollowed out portions that animate and lighten them. The paint job extends right to the bottom of the body and creates the optical illusion that it is closer to the ground than it is. From the front, it is dominated by the large trapezoidal air intake that serves the radiator and the engine bay. The two lower intakes, for the brakes, are elements that model the spoiler. The dimensions, rather than the presence of elements of design, lend great importance to the hood, in which the retractable headlamps are lightly marked by two ribs. The side panels draw attention to the air vents of the engine bay. The roof is well connected to the tail and the rear has a very convex shape, underlined by its sharp upper edge. It houses two circular groups of lights. But that great sense of compactness, which makes its outline so fascinating, does not prevent the interior from being extremely comfortable."

The opportunity to upholster the interior of the finest custom-built car ever to be mass produced arose when Frau Car

had already demonstrated its abilities on cars produced by companies like Lancia, BMW, Nissan and Mercedes. By curious coincidence, Bruno Sacco, responsible for Mercedes design over the last two decades of the twentieth century, spent his youth in the creative atmosphere of the body builders of Turin, and thus came into contact with Pininfarina, Bertone and Giugiaro. "For twenty years I have followed two basic lines at Mercedes," he told me in an interview published in *Abitare* no. 391, of January 2000: "Presenting models similar in style (horizontal consistency), which means that any Mercedes is recognizable as such, and always trying to make the evolutionary origin of the latest development apparent (vertical affinity). This makes it possible to immediately recognize the family to which the model belongs, its parents and grandparents. Thus I have pursued the goal of a production in which the models that are gradually replaced do not run the risk of looking outmoded, but serve instead as guarantees of evolutionary continuity." Poltrona Frau has produced classic leather-upholstered interiors for the most classic of Mercedes. However, in re-forging the link with the automobile world of Turin, which Renzo had established in the early years of the twentieth century, Franco Moschini laid the foundations for a lasting col-

The Frau Car division has upholstered the interiors of some of the most prestigious products of the international automobile industry. Examples include the BMW series 5, series 3 and series 3 convertible and (on facing page) the Mercedes 350 SL.

At the age of seventy-seven the American astronaut John Glenn returns to space aboard the *Discovery*, 1998. Touch armchair, designed by Jean Nouvel, 1998. "Smooth but soft as well, round but taut too, free of any superfluous element and, at the same time, sincere, Touch evokes the sensation of kissing, of melting, but makes a deep impression by its simplicity and by the way it appears to yearn for intimacy."

laboration with the FIAT Group. After the 456 GT of 1992, it would be the turn of the 550 Maranello of 1996 and of the most recent fruit of the synergy between Pininfarina and Ferrari, the 370 Modena of 1999. A production line set up for the purpose, in the automobile upholstery department of Poltrona Frau, continues to fulfill orders for those red Ferraris, the most beautiful cars on the world, for which Frau Car now guarantees the quality of the leather where the Prancing Horse had previously relied on refined British tanneries. The excellence of the leather and the upholstery only add to the quality of the whole automobile, in which the sensual and alluring interior offers emotional gratification even before the vehicle is set in motion, roaring off to demonstrate its full dynamic potential.

The year 1998, however, also saw the birth of Jean Nouvel's Touch, a system of seating for the community whose motivations are summed up in exemplary fashion by the design-

er himself. "It is through contact with the hands, and above all the body, that objects become familiar and pleasing. This allows us to tame them. Tactile perception, today, comes into collision with the despotism of the image. Touch represents the victory of sensuality, associated with the force of leather. There is something of the animal, muscular and energetic, about this force. The elimination of edges, of seams, creates a continuity that is reminiscent of the caress. Smooth but soft as well, round but taut too, free of any superfluous element and, at the same time, sincere, Touch evokes the sensation of kissing, of melting, but makes a deep impression by its simplicity and by the way it appears to yearn for intimacy. It is an attraction complementary to the body, the same as you feel toward your favorite clothes." In his extolling of tactile perception, Jean Nouvel rightly celebrates its physicality, in opposition to the despotic sidestepping of that very quality. "'Today the velocity of the ear and the eye has taken the

Touch at the Poltrona Frau stand of the Salone del Mobile in Milan, 1999.

place of perception, of human response, so the coupling of audiovisual velocity and instantaneity of response carries along with it all the effects of a drug, which are not simply those of chemical hallucinogens, but hallucinatory effects induced by different types of audiovisual products.' For some time, Paul Virilio has been warning of the perils of the virtual approach which is gradually replacing contact with reality," commented the author of this book in *Agorà* no. 20, September 1997. "Especially when the subject, no longer a spectator and therefore aware that he is watching a spectacle, is even induced to take part, to become an actor in rela-

tion to the prefigured landscape." As Jean Nouvel says: "It is through contact with the hands, and above all the body, that objects become familiar and pleasing. This allows us to tame them."

Tactile experience opposes this dangerous negation of the senses, and is therefore the best way to define the peculiarities of Touch, ideally suited to its location in community settings where it is possible to formulate liberating proposals at a time when both work and leisure have fallen under the sway of technological devices. As the presentation puts it: "Here Jean Nouvel places the accent on the tactile relation-

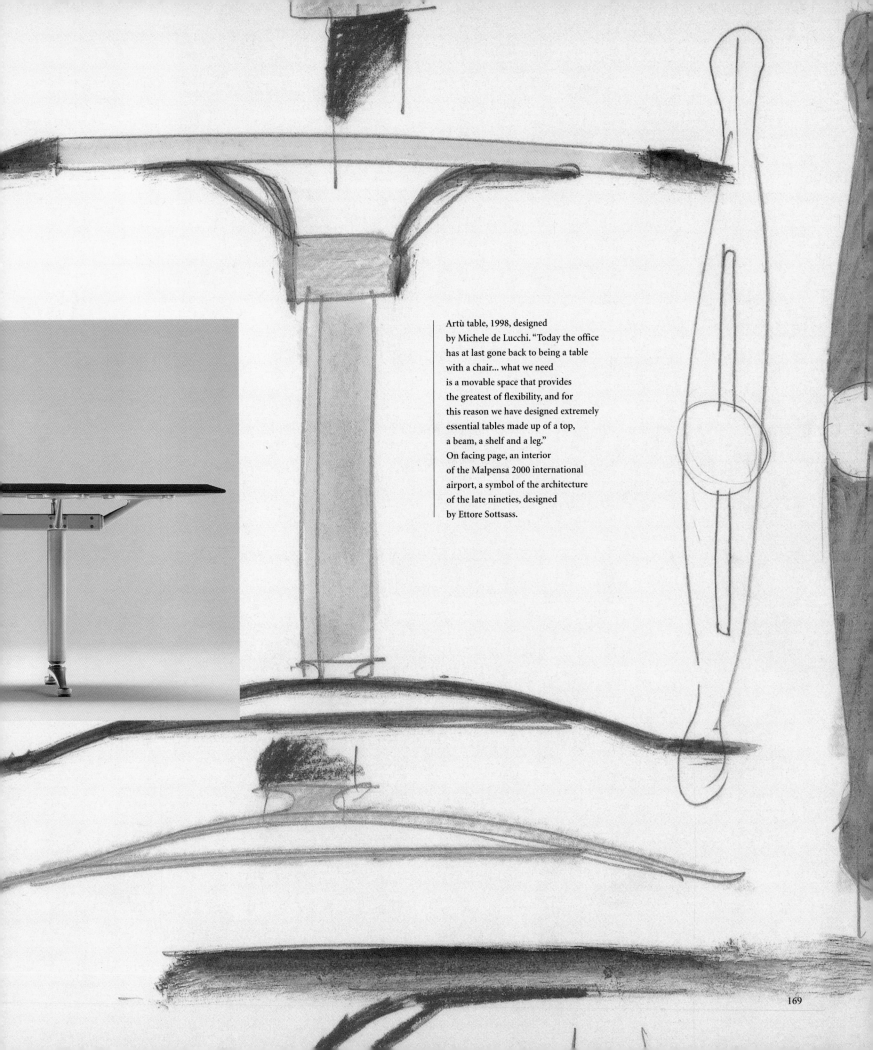

Artù table, 1998, designed
by Michele de Lucchi. "Today the office
has at last gone back to being a table
with a chair... what we need
is a movable space that provides
the greatest of flexibility, and for
this reason we have designed extremely
essential tables made up of a top,
a beam, a shelf and a leg."
On facing page, an interior
of the Malpensa 2000 international
airport, a symbol of the architecture
of the late nineties, designed
by Ettore Sottsass.

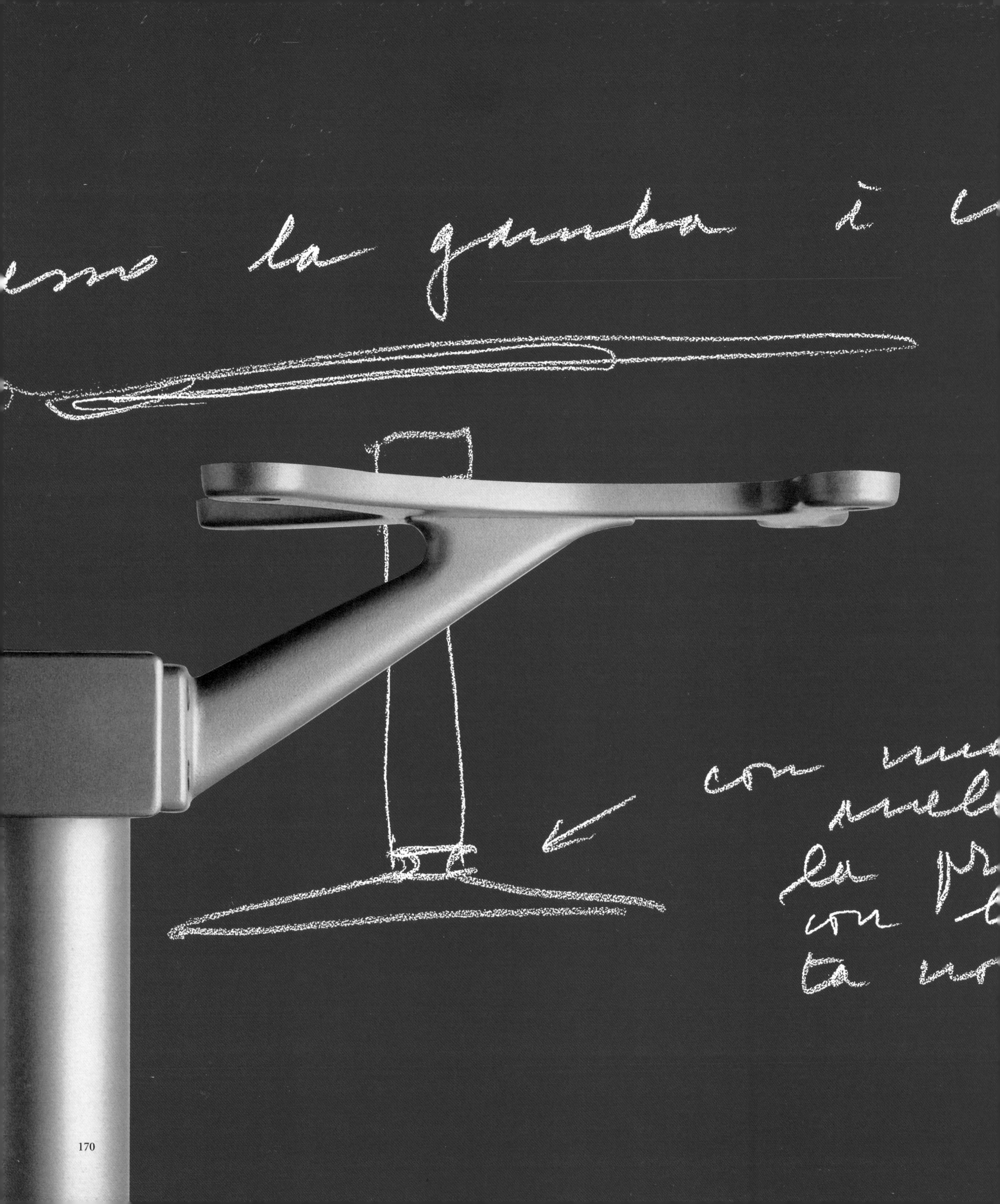
la gamba
con

ship between the body and the upholstery with its taut leather covering. It represents an attempt on his part to challenge the tyranny of the visual and the immaterial and to restore the supremacy of the sense of touch. So from the linguistic viewpoint Touch can be seen as a reaffirmation of sensuality, closely connected with the almost muscular tension of the leather. The elimination of edges and even of visible seams also creates a continuity of form that produces the pleasant sensation of a caress. Soft and smooth, rounded and taut, essential and warm, Touch invites you to sit on it and adopt a comfortable position."

Thus Jean Nouvel's aim was to impart the sense of a velvety soft caress to his system of seats, which can be combined in a harmonious way to create a place for relaxation and reflection. By contrast, Michele de Lucchi's Artù range of furniture, also from 1998, was concerned with the community in its working dimension. And de Lucchi was well aware that what is understood by the place of work today is a computerized workstation. They are used by the porter at the door and by the company president, however different their roles may be. So he decided to propose, as an alternative, a place for sharing, for the exclusive face-to-face meeting, excluding the mediation of telecommunications: Artù, named after Arthur, the legendary leader of Roman and British resistance to the invasion of the Saxons around the middle of the first millennium. The literary echo of his mythical exploits resounded right through the Middle Ages and came to form the so-called Arthurian legend. Arthur's knights used to gather around the famous round table. Michele de Lucchi set out to re-create the sense of complicity that arises when several people sit shoulder to shoulder and each person meets the gaze of the person opposite. All they have in common is the surface on which they rest their elbows, the shared territory of creative tension and decision-making. In this sense de Lucchi, like Jean Nouvel, assumes the supremacy of the senses over the despotism of the image. "In recent years," writes Hans Hoger in Artù, "a growing number of people are discovering the renewed importance of the physical place... The center of this type of place, the point of reference for communication and meeting, is the table. It is the object we sit at in order to concentrate. It is the central element of the room, where we invite other people to talk, discuss, analyze and speculate.

1999: Roberto Benigni receiving the Oscar for Best Performance by an Actor in a Leading Role and Best Foreign Language Film for *La vita è bella*.
On facing page, study sketches by Michele de Lucchi for the Artù project.

The new millennium opens:
festivities and fireworks in London.
Donald chair, designed
by Pierluigi Cerri, 2000.

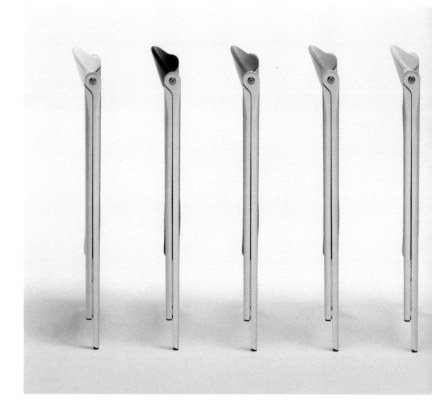

Digital media have not made face-to-face communication obsolete. On the contrary, the digital revolution has only served to increase our need for places where we can get together with other people, to bring things up to date, to define strategies and make presentations, to organize workshops and check information, to put forward ideas... What dominates in Artù is a sort of gentle engineering, coupled with precise proportions and formal interventions (the structure on which the top rests almost weightlessly, the lines of the legs and feet, the fiber-optic lighting elements, the joints between wood and metal in the shape of a chameleon's claw), that impart a surprising and subtle figurative quality to the design."

And Silvana Suardi, again in *Artù*: "In effect, when seated around a table, we find ourselves at the center of a web of relations, activities and plans that fill the space and lend meaning to it. A space that, today especially, is perceived in a mutable way and that has value to the extent that relations are capable of developing in it… 'Today the office has at last gone back to being a table with a chair,' says Michele de Lucchi, and "what we need is a movable space that provides the greatest of flexibility, and for this reason we have designed extremely essential tables made up of a top, a beam, a shelf and a leg."

In contrast to relationships handled through the medium of telecommunications, direct, one-on-one communication between people is founded on simplicity, though not on simplification, for design in relation to the human being is always a complex matter. "An interesting characteristic of aluminum," comments Michele de Lucchi, "here used in the extruded form although part is die-cast, is that it can be coated. We experimented with a version veneered with cherry wood as well as one covered with leather, closer to the Frau conception of furniture. This permits the combination of materials to attain a sophisticated customization of individual solutions. "I find the theme of the conference or meeting table even more fascinating today now that the workplace has to be seen in terms of the encounter between people, and that this can be in more than one place, even places that are a long way from one another. I am thinking of locations where a high degree of professionalism, a high concentration of knowledge, is involved. So the table can be extended or reduced in size in relation to the number of people who are going to sit at it and meet face to face." And here de Lucchi is referring to the ancient sense of setting the

Its profile recalls the eye and beak of the famous duck. Donald is a three hundred and sixty degree seat, the full circle of the compass from which its function of opening and closing is derived.

table, when the top, cut from the heartwood of a tree, usually oak, was prepared for the occasion and set on a piece of wood or quarry stone or sandstone that raised it above the ground to a height where people could sit at it. The ritual of preparation of the table, always temporary, was divided into two phases: setting and clearing. Increasingly, the action became confined to the top of the tables, while the support was made permanent. Yet de Lucchi affirms the urgency of sharing, which must not be a question of habit, but of construction, of preparation in the most suitable manner for each occasion, as determined by the need of the moment. So that being elbow to elbow, face to face, is now an indispensable physical necessity.

"The image has become the world," warns Paul Virilio in *Appuntamenti con la filosofia*. "Images shape the world, they are imprisoning it. The surface of the world is perfectly familiar to us thanks to satellites, but the images that help us to see the world have become just as unfamiliar as the world they have revealed. The unknown has shifted: from a world that was too vast, mysterious and wild, it has moved into images, which

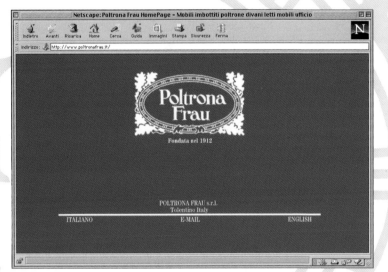

have become too big, too disturbing... There are few explorers who analyze them, though many may start out doing so. Scientists, artists, philosophers... We all find ourselves in a sort of 'new alliance' to explore this nebula of the image. The image only ever exists in relation to a recognized reality. And a reality is a shared language. If we are not in the same reality we cannot communicate. Each of us has one bit of it, but nobody understands that that bit has to be put into the common pot so that we can arrive at an understanding. This is what happened in the Renaissance, a phenomenon in which everybody took part. In addition to being an organization of the city, a geometricization, the Renaissance was above all an organization of vision." Thus the intention behind the design of Artù is preparation, according to need, of the place best suited to making it possible to share, to renew the "alliance," as Virilio puts it. And the Artù range is once again a mode of Frau living, inasmuch as it is craftsmanship that ensures that the advanced technological solu-

tions involved in its manufacture are suited to the needs of the human being. A process in which, consequently, technology is not pursued for its own sake, but is a means of constant improvement.

And this brings us neatly to the most recent of Frau's offspring: Pierluigi Cerri's Donald, brought out in 2000.

Its profile recalls the eye and beak of the famous duck. Donald is a three hundred and sixty degree seat, the full circle of the compass from which its function of opening and closing is derived. Thus it is not a fixed layout, arranged for a certain number of guests, but a comfortable seat that adapts to the need of the occasion, when an unexpected guest arrives to close the circle of sharing. Hence it is not designed for a particular place, but is itself a place in relation to the other places in which we live, from the home to the public space. And in this sense Donald too is a worthy heir to that philosophy of the product ushered in by Renzo Frau: the function must always served by a comfortable form, completely free of any deference to mannered eclecticism. However, its identity is already evident, as the fruit of accomplished research, in the handling of the materials: die-cast aluminum, for the structure, is combined with steel for the inlays; expanded thermoplastic resin, is used for the padding of seat and back; leather in the shades of the Color System and leather is used to cover and enhance the form. There can be no doubt that, today, Hermann Muthesius would not have written about the model house, with particular reference to one country, but about the voices that come together, at an international level, to create the most suitable type of furnishing, perhaps founding their research on an attempt at mediation between artisan culture and technological evolution.

In this sense, he would not be able to ignore Poltrona Frau, especially today, as an example of an approach to design which makes the awareness of the craftsman responsible for the technological evolution of furniture upholstered in leather, in all its forms, forms which represent exclusive modes of living.

o. 10141757

Index of Poltrona Frau Illustrations

Bibliography

LIBRARY
D.I.T. MOUNTJOY SQ.

Antonetto, R. *Torino l'altro ieri*, Priuli & Verlucca, Ivrea 1976

Argan, G.C. "L'arte e la tecnologia moderna," in Nardi P. (edited by), *Arte e cultura nella civiltà contemporanea*, Sansoni, Florence 1966

Atlante storico Garzanti: cronologia della storia universale, Garzanti, Milan 1994

Atlante storico, Garzanti, Milan 1997

Baroni, D. *Frau. Un nome, una poltrona, una storia*, edizioni Poltrona Frau, Tolentino 1990; *Bello quotidiano*, edizioni Federlegno Arredo, Milan 1995; *La collezione Hydra*, edizioni Poltrona Frau, Tolentino 1992; *Caruso roof-garden*, edizioni Poltrona Frau, Tolentino 1991

Barthes, R. *Mythologies* [undated]

Bassani, G. *The Garden of the Finzi Continis*, Harcourt, Inc., New York 1980

Battaglia, S. *Grande dizionario della lingua italiana*, Utet, Turin 1961

Bianciardi, L. *L'integrazione*, Bompiani, Milan 1960

Binaghi, R.M. "Regesto," in *Torino città viva da capitale a metropoli 1880-1980*, Centro Studi Piemontese, Turin 1980

Borgna, G. *Storia della canzone italiana*, Mondadori, Milan 1992

Boscolo, A. (edited by), *Viaggiatori dell'Ottocento in Sardegna*, Editrice Sarda Fossataro, Cagliari 1973

Bosoni, G. in Gregotti, V. *Il disegno del prodotto industriale: Italia 1860-1980*, Electa, Milan 1998

Burkhardt, F. *Marco Zanuso*, Motta, Milan 1994

Caballo, E. *Pininfarina. Nato con l'automobile*, Palazzi, Milan 1968

Caorsi, G. "Il cinema," in *Torino città viva da capitale a metropoli 1880-1980*, Centro Studi Piemontese, Turin 1980

Carena, G. *Prontuario di vocaboli attenenti a parecchie arti, ad alcuni mestieri, a cose domestiche, e altre di uso comune*, Stamperia Reale, Turin 1851

Carugati, D.G.R. *Pininfarina. Identity of a Design*, Electa, Milan 1999; *Agorà*, no. 20, September 1997; *Intervista*, Politi, November 1997; "La Porsche, evoluzione e design," in *Abitare*, no. 379, 1998; *Abitare*, no. 391, January 2000

Cherchi Usai, P.(edited by), *Giovanni Pastrone*, Utet, Turin 1986

Chigiotti, G. "Il progetto: un ideale a quattro mani," in *Sergio Mazza e Giuliana Gramigna. Quarant'anni di professione*, Maschietto e Musolino, Florence-Siena 1995

Conti, F. *Tito Agnoli*, Rima, Milan 1988

Cortesi, A. *Letteratura e Scienza, le poetiche del design*, I Dispari, Milan 1995

D'Annunzio, G. *Del cinematografo considerato come strumento di liberazione e come arte di trasfigurazione*, 1914: text reproduced in Cherchi Usai, P. (edited by) *Giovanni Pastrone*, courtesy of Fondazione Il Vittoriale degli Italiani, Utet, Turin 1986; *L'innocente*, Mondadori, Milan 1940

De Lucchi, M. *Artù*, edizioni Poltrona Frau, Tolentino 1999

Del Bosco, P. *Fonografo italiano 1890-1940*, Nuova Fonit Cetra [undated]

De Mattia, G. in Baroni, D. (edited by), *Il Teatro Lauro Rossi*, edizioni Comune di Macerata, Macerata 1989

De Pisis, F. "I ranoni," in *La città dalle cento meraviglie*, Vallecchi, Florence 1965

Devoto, G. & Oli, G. *Dizionario della lingua italiana*, Le Monnier, Florence 1973

Eco, U. "Il concetto comico," in *I boss media*, Editori Riuniti, Rome 1969

Enciclopedia di filosofia, Garzanti, Milan 1998

Enciclopedia della letteratura, Garzanti, Milan 1997

Ferranti, P. *Poltrona Frau*, degree thesis, Faculty of Architecture in Florence, Florence 1988–89

Flitch Crawford, J.E. "Cagliari, Oristano, Tharros," in Boscolo A. (edited by), *Viaggiatori dell'Ottocento in Sardegna*, translation by F. Alziator, Editrice Sarda Fossataro, Cagliari 1973

Frere, P. *Porsche 911*, translation by D. Biffignandi, Nada, Milan 1994

Garzoni, T. *La piazza universale di tutte le professioni del mondo*, edited by P. Cherchi and B. Collina, Einaudi, Turin 1996

Goncarov, I. *Oblomov*, translation by E. Lo Gatto, Einaudi, Turin 1979

Gozzano, G. *Le poesie, La via del rifugio, I colloqui, Le farfalle, Poesie sparse*, edited by E. Sanguineti, Einaudi, Turin 1973 and 1990

Gregotti V., *Il disegno del prodotto industriale: Italia 1860-1980*, Electa, Milan 1998

Hoger, H. in *Artù*, edizioni Poltrona Frau, Tolentino 1999

Joyce, J. *Ulysses*, Penguin Books, Harmondsworth 1960

Lenci, F. interview in *Casa Oggi*, no. 159, September 1987

Maimeri, G. *Diari*, Charta, Milan 1996

Mang, K. *The History of Modern Furniture*, Academy Editions, London 1979

Marangoni, G. "Glorie ed evoluzioni della poltrona," in *La cultura moderna*, no. 2, February 1929

Mereghetti, P. *Dizionario dei film 1998*, Baldini & Castoldi, Milan 1997

Meucci, A. *La Sardegna nelle pagine di uno scrittore inglese*, Arti Grafiche Lazzeri, Siena 1918

Minoli, P. interview in *Casa Oggi*, no. 159, September 1987

Moravia A., *The Time of Indifference*, Penguin Books, Harmondworth 1970

Mulas A., *The Getty Center*, edizioni Poltrona Frau, Tolentino 1998

Nouvel, J. *Touch, dichiarazione di pugno*, Paris 1999

Numero, July 1915, Turin

La nuova enciclopedia dell'arte, Garzanti, Milan 1997

La nuova enciclopedia della musica, Garzanti, Milan 1992

Palazzeschi, A. "L'incendiario," in *Stampe dell'Ottocento*, Vallecchi, Florence 1943

Pansera, A. *Storia del disegno industriale italiano*, Laterza, Rome-Bari 1993; *Luigi Massoni. Il pioniere della via marchigiana al design*, Loreto Arte, 1999

Piovene, G. *Madame la France*, Mondadori, Milan 1966

Ponti, G. in *Domus*, no. 440, 1966

Porsche, F.A., interview in *Casa Oggi*, no. 159, September 1987

Ramorino, F. *Mitologia classica*, Hoepli, Milan 1934

Savinio, A. *Casa La vita*, Adelphi, Milan 1988

Sbarbaro, C. *Scampoli*, Vallecchi, Florence 1960

Sgorlon, C. *La poltrona*, Mondadori, Milan 1968

Suardi, S. in *Artù*, edizioni Poltrona Frau, Tolentino 1999

Tesio, G. "Le lettere," in *Torino città viva da capitale a metropoli 1880-1980*, Centro Studi Piemontese, Turin 1980

Tomizza, F. *L'amicizia*, Rizzoli, Milan 1980

Tonelli Michail, M.C. *Il design in Italia 1925-1943*, Laterza, Rome-Bari 1987

Tozzi, F. *Con gli occhi chiusi*, Einaudi, Turin 1988

Treccani. *Dizionario enciclopedico*, Rome [undated]

Ungaretti, G. *L'allegria*, Mondadori, Milan 1970

Virilio, P. in *Appuntamenti con la filosofia*, Politi, Milan 1989

Vuiller, G.C. "Città e paesi," in Boscolo, A. (edited by), *Viaggiatori dell'Ottocento in Sardegna*, translation by F. Alziator, Editrice Sarda Fossataro, Cagliari 1973